I0530859

THE LIGHT
I COULDN'T
NAME

How I Learned to See, Name,
and Love My Autistic Self

Serena Poganski

Copyright © 2025 by Serena Poganski

All rights reserved. No part of this publication may be reproduced, stored in a retrieval system, or transmitted in any form or by any means—electronic, mechanical, photocopying, recording, or otherwise—without the prior written permission of the publisher, except for brief quotations used in reviews or scholarly works.

This is a work of nonfiction. While every effort has been made to present events truthfully, some names, identifying details, and circumstances have been changed to protect the privacy of individuals. Any resemblance to actual persons, living or dead, is purely coincidental unless otherwise stated.

The information presented in this book is based on the author's personal experiences and research. It is not intended as a substitute for professional medical, psychological, or educational advice. Readers are encouraged to consult qualified professionals regarding their own situations.

Contents

Prologue

A few things about me (before we get into the deep stuff):

- I'm trained in understanding human behavior, yet I still rehearse every conversation in my head like it's opening night.

- I'm a wife and a mom of two boys, which means my life is a solid blend of deep love, sensory overload, and the occasional retreat to the closet for five minutes of silence.

- I love writing—it gives my thoughts somewhere to go when speaking out loud feels too clumsy.

- I hate the sound of chewing. Like, viscerally. I will leave the room to prevent myself from imploding.

- I can analyze someone's emotional patterns with ease, but small talk gives me existential dread.

- When it comes to food, I have texture trust issues. One weird bite and we're done forever.

- Lists are like lifeboats for me. Creating them brings order to my tangled thoughts, and crossing things off gives me the most satisfying little dopamine hit.

- My memory is sharp in unexpected ways. I'll recall exact moments from years ago but lose track of what I'm saying mid-sentence.

- I take comfort in familiar routines and sensory experiences—like soft fabrics, quiet evenings, and my favorite cup of coffee.

- I tend to be quiet in groups, but my mind is always running—analyzing, imagining, remembering.

- I love deeply, feel everything too much, and sometimes wish the world came with a volume knob.

- I'm autistic. I didn't always know. Now that I do, everything finally makes sense.

Introduction

Sharing that I am autistic with others is always a gamble—I'm never quite sure what sort of response I'm going to get. It's typically either an exclamation of disbelief, something like, "No way! You seem pretty normal to me," or I'm met with a sympathetic, uncomfortable silence, as if I'd just told them I've got some awful illness.

I try to give people the benefit of the doubt. There was a time when I didn't fully understand what it meant to be autistic either. I never imagined that autism would one day become such a significant part of my identity—or that I'd feel so strongly about advocating, educating, and breaking down the stigma surrounding it. But here I am, sharing what I've learned, woven within my own unique story.

The range of autistic experiences is vast, yet the media often narrows it down to two contrasting images: the non-speaking white male with a train fixation who reacts violently to stress, and the highly intelligent, almost encyclopedic genius.

While those profiles do exist and deserve recognition, they're not nearly the full picture. Sometimes autism is female.

Sometimes it's someone who blends in so well with the neurotypical world that no one notices the contradictions between their outside behavior and internal experience.[1]

I'm what you call "high masking," which essentially means that I'm a very good actor. I can suppress my autistic traits in order to blend in and appear neurotypical. I tend to put on a mask more when I'm at work, around unfamiliar people, or when I feel vulnerable. I unmask when I feel fully accepted and comfortable—which doesn't happen easily or often.

What does this look like in practice? When I'm masking, I force myself to make eye contact even when it feels uncomfortable. I sit still when my body wants to move. I smile and act easygoing, even though inside I'm micromanaging every detail. When I'm unmasked, you might catch me fidgeting, blurting nonsense words that feel good to my brain, freaking out over last-minute changes, or rambling on about a special interest for far longer than what's socially "appropriate."

It's normal, of course, to adjust your behavior depending on the setting, like avoiding curse words in front of your boss. But living your whole life as a chameleon, constantly shifting to meet others' expectations, takes a toll. In fact, recent research shows a correlation between high masking scores on the CAT-Q, a self-report screening tool for social camouflaging behaviors, and a lower overall quality of life.[2]

After realizing how negatively masking has been impacting my confidence and well-being, I embarked on my journey of learning how to unmask. Writing this book has been one part of that journey.

Reducing the stigma surrounding autism is key to helping high-masking autistic people live more freely. Why is it we aren't afraid to talk about feeling overstimulated or being a "highly sensitive person," yet the word "autism" can feel so dirty?

The truth is, the world remains critically undereducated about autism. Here's some perspective: the first person ever diagnosed with autism, Donald Triplett, passed away only recently—in 2023, at the age of 89.[3] That's how young our collective understanding still is.

My hope is that by sharing both my story and my personal research, this book will help clarify what it really means to be neurodivergent in a neurotypical world. I want to celebrate brain diversity, not rank it.

I hope this reaches suspecting autistics who are curious, newly discovered autistics who are on their own journeys of self exploration, loved ones who are so selflessly seeking understanding, and just about everyone else—because every person, autistic or not, deserves to be accepted and appreciated for who they really are.

Don't Worry, She's Just Shy

Being a "good girl" covered a lot of ground: quiet, polite, obedient, adaptable. For a while, it worked. But it also kept people from asking the right questions—and kept me from understanding myself.

Since I didn't receive my autism diagnosis until adulthood, I've spent a lot of time looking back on my childhood for clues—subtle signs that autism was always there, lurking behind the "shy girl" label I wore like a name tag. Because let's face it: if you were a girl growing up in the '90s, you couldn't possibly be autistic. (And just in case you're a literal-thinking autistic like me—yes, that was sarcasm.) Back then, autism was still largely viewed as a "male disorder." If you were quiet and well-behaved, as many autistic girls tend to be, you were just seen as shy. If, on the other hand, you were disruptive or made life harder for teachers or caregivers, then autism might come into the conversation.

The reason that autism is frequently missed in girls is that they are generally more adept at observing and mirroring the social behaviors of those around them, leading to a less obvious presentation. They're also more expected to do so than their male counterparts. "Be a lady." "Use your manners." That's what we were taught. But boys? Well, boys will be boys...right?

The problem is that autism often goes unnoticed until it inconveniences someone else. By the time that happens, the autistic person has likely spent far too long in an environment that doesn't align with their needs. What people often label as "severe behaviors" aren't really symptoms of autism itself—they're distress signals. They're signs of unmet needs, misunderstandings, or a lack of proper accommodations.

And it's not just girls who are missed. Even boys who don't exhibit serious disruptive behaviors are often diagnosed later than those who outwardly struggle.[1] That's why it's so important to understand the many different ways autism can present across genders, ages, and personality types.

People described me as both painfully shy and exceptionally bright when I was a young girl. My mother tells me I began speaking in full sentences before the age of one, and for a long time, I didn't believe her. I just chalked it up to a proud-mom exaggeration. But after diving into research on autism in females, I discovered that being hyperverbal from an early age is quite common. A 2018 study found that infants at high risk for autism spectrum disorder produced significantly more vocalizations than their low-risk peers.[2]

Since the diagnostic criteria for autism include social and communication challenges, this finding seems contradicting. However, while the research found the overall frequency of vocalizations to be higher in high-risk infants, they also found that this same group engaged in significantly less *reciprocal* babbling, meaning fewer back-and-forth exchanges with adults. In other words, they made more sounds, but showed early differences in social communication.

Of course, this isn't always the case. The more stereotypical view is that autistic individuals are late to speak or may never speak at all. Speech delays are common in autism, especially among boys, but they can occur in girls as well.[3] Still, the inverse is also true: many autistic children speak early, and some even develop advanced language or reading skills before their peers. I was one of them. I was also an early reader, a trait known as hyperlexia, which is frequently associated with autism.[4]

I remember being fascinated by letters at a very young age, eagerly reading signs from the backseat during car rides. One oddly vivid memory I have is walking into a CVS and spotting the giant red letters on the floor: C-V-S. I must have been thrilled, because I brought it up to my mom recently, and she remembered it too. Apparently, my excitement made an impression.

Despite my early language skills, I began to hide my ability to speak once I became consciously aware of the people around me. I recall whispering into my mom's ear so she could speak for me, especially around unfamiliar adults. In hindsight, others probably assumed my mom was exaggerating when she claimed

I was highly verbal—because I certainly didn't act that way in public. Strangers were terrifying to me.

During my first preschool experience, teachers noticed something different about me. One even suggested to my mom that I might be on the spectrum because of my social difficulties. But like so many parents at the time, she only understood the most stereotypical version of autism—non-speaking boys with clear cognitive delays—so she dismissed the idea and pulled me out of the school.

My mom was relieved to find a Montessori school where they reassured her I'd be okay, describing me as just a shy, cautious child. I still had difficulty separating from my mom, still didn't talk in public, and still didn't know how to make friends. I remember feeling anxious, uncomfortable, and confused, especially during free, unstructured play. I have a distinct memory of wandering around in circles during free play when a teacher approached and said, "Serena, you have one minute to find something to do." I panicked and quickly chose the nearest activity to avoid further confrontation.

Eventually, I was "assigned" a friend. When my teacher noticed that I spent most of my time on the playground standing near the adults instead of playing with other kids, she paired me with the most outgoing, friendly little girl in the class. Her name was Brooke—and I adored her.

For the first time, I didn't feel so alone or confused. Brooke took my hand and pulled me gently into her world. She led me into her play group, and by following her lead, I slowly began learning how to blend in with the other girls. She became my anchor, my source of safety and predictability. Every morning, she was there when my mom dropped me off, and I clung to her side for the rest of the day.

My time at Montessori was my first small taste of what it felt like to move through the world without the comfort of the familiar to hide behind. It pushed me to use my voice, if only a little, and dropped me into a social environment I had to actively work to adapt to. It wasn't easy. I still spent more time observing than interacting with other kids. It was also the first time I remember feeling genuinely confused by how naturally everyone else seemed to know how to join in. That part just didn't come to me like it did others.

Fast forward to primary school, I was still extremely shy and still attached myself to adults over other children, but I slowly gained bits of confidence and made some friends over time. In second grade, I met my best friend to this day. Sadie was an outgoing, funny kid who helped immensely with getting me to come out of my shell. At home, I was already pretty goofy and fun-loving when I felt comfortable, and she made me feel like I could be that version of myself around her, too. She, like Brooke, had a carefree spirit and readily adopted me as her friend. She spoke her mind and owned her uniqueness. Throughout my whole life, I've been drawn to such people. Perhaps it's because I admire those who feel no need to become small or appear ordinary, despite being so obviously rare in nature.

Sadie and I attended the same private school together for several years, and by 6th grade, I had swung from one extreme to the other. We were a pair of obnoxious chatterboxes, constantly disrupting class with our giggling fits and getting separated as a result. I guess you could say my mask came off, and I became me, and then some.

We passed notes all day, created imaginary worlds together, and laughed until chocolate milk came out of our noses. We were a package deal—if you knew one of us, you knew the other. Being around Sadie meant I could be unapologetically myself. That version of me was eccentric, unconventional, and often "too much" for people. Sadie was the same, in her own ways. So we were either loved or loathed—rarely anything in between. But because we had each other, it didn't matter.

After middle school, I transferred to a different private school that was closer to home and a bit more relaxed than the last. I was especially excited to be done with uniforms—those stiff, button-down shirts made from itchy fabric felt like the bane of my existence.

Part of me wanted a fresh start. While I had Sadie, I didn't have many other close friends. I'd been in the same small class since first grade, and by the time high school rolled around, I was already typecast: the odd one out. I didn't fit neatly into the group's social dynamics, and everyone seemed to have decided who I was.

I wondered if I'd find new friends at my new school, where I'd have the chance to enter the picture with a new reputation—one that would make me seem more likeable. At my old school, I'd become known as weird, annoying, even unapproachable. That was because I was so unfiltered around Sadie. I no longer wore a mask.

My plan was to start over—to be more friendly, more talkative, more "normal." And so on the first day of high school, I walked through those unfamiliar doors wearing the mask I thought I'd left behind years earlier.

I didn't adapt at all like I had somehow expected. Initially, the "cool kids" seemed to think that I fit into their group, at least based on how I looked. They eagerly invited me to sit with them, and it made me feel good—at first.

But I quickly grew tired of the constant gossip and endless talk about pop culture, none of which interested me. I had no idea how to join their conversations, so I mostly sat there in silence, waiting to be asked a question. The more I held back, the less they tried to get to know me, and the less welcome I felt.

At some point or another, I migrated to a different group—one that didn't care about status or appearance. And honestly, it was much more interesting. My challenges with joining into conversations were still... challenging, but I had something to work with. Over the years (yes, it took years), I gained a few close friends. Looking back, I'm almost certain that some or most of them were also neurodivergent. They all had their own quirks, special interests, and rocky mental health. What can I say? Relatable.

Meanwhile, the original group that had so eagerly welcomed me stopped being nice. I'd unknowingly become known as the quiet, artsy girl with a perpetually unimpressed expression. The mask had slipped again. Sure, I kept to myself, but that didn't justify the whispers, the sideways glances, or the sarcastic remarks that started showing up in place of kindness.

"Why don't you ever talk?"

"Why are you sad all the time?"

"You look miserable."

I'm sure the things said to my face were the nicer ones. I'd heard some of the horrible things that were said about my friends behind their backs, and they were much less tame.

Over time, the way they saw me started to shape how I saw myself. I began to wonder if something was wrong with me. Why was it so hard to open up to people? Why didn't I ever seem to know the right things to say, the questions to ask, the secret to connection?

Half of me wanted to fit in with the typical crowd; the other half didn't care. I think I just wanted to know what it felt like to belong without having to try so hard—without having to perform. But eventually, partway through the school year, I gave up on trying.

Academics, at least, were a little more straightforward. I thrived in subjects like English and writing, but math was another story (which just goes to show, not every autistic person is a math genius). I did well in any class that relied on memorization. I'd skim through my notes the morning of a quiz or test and still recall things easily. But ask me to calculate something? Forget it.

The arts—music theory, choir, drawing, and painting—also interested me. And yes, I was a theater kid too. That one always surprises people, given my quiet and reserved demeanor.

My mom encouraged me to get involved with a local theater production around age 12. She thought it would help me with my shyness and with making new friends. It stuck and became a huge passion throughout my childhood and teen years.

The thing about performing is that there's always a script—always a plan. There are rehearsals, cues, blocking. There's structure. And for someone like me, that structure was incredibly comforting. As funny as it sounds, it has always been easier for me to perform for a large audience or deliver a memorized speech than to navigate a small, casual conversation. Conversation is unscripted. It's improv. And ask me to do improv? I'll freeze. I'll panic. I'll overthink every word.

Because of how much I thrived in the world of theater, it became a very strong interest of mine from the beginning, and a source of safety for me throughout all of middle school and high school. I was almost always involved in some sort of production at a local theater that was, by some sort of great luck, only five minutes from my home. Like every interest I've ever had, it was all I could think about at the time. Each show became my world. I'd have every song, every monologue—often every line in the entire script—memorized without even trying. After school, I'd go to rehearsals and retreat to worlds where I could play a role and really emerge from my quiet shell.

Everything about theater brought me joy: the creative expression, the stories told through music, the shared purpose with other performers. Yet when I dig deeper, I also know that an even bigger reason for my love of theater was that it was the *one* place where I felt fully confident in the spotlight, a place where I was no longer me, but a curated character.

But of course, high school ended, and real life didn't come with scripts. While most of the seniors I graduated with carefully selected their "perfect" universities based on things like culture, status, and extracurriculars, I took a different route. I chose to start at a community college so I could continue working and move at a slower, more manageable pace. I had zero interest in the social scene. I just wanted to learn and figure out a career path I could feel passionate about.

I initially wanted to pursue something related to writing or music, two of the things that drew me in the most at the time. But when I started looking at things like job prospects and average salaries, I felt the need to be practical. Passions can be hobbies, I told myself. I needed something more "realistic."

So, I jumped straight to careers in business. *I'll try out accounting!* I thought. I could keep to myself. It would make me look smart. There are even remote opportunities. I thought I'd made the perfect choice—spreadsheets, consistency, independence, and quiet.

Well... let's just say I'm about as far from being an accountant as you can get. (Spoiler: it did not go well—but that's a story for another chapter.)

New Surroundings, Old Sensitivities

Following my time at the community college, I made the decision to transfer to a university about an hour's drive from my home with my parents, where I still lived. I was set on getting my Bachelor's degree in accounting—the money would be good, I'd be able to work in my own cubicle with minimal pressure to socialize, and I was starting to find this strange satisfaction in the balancing of numbers on a spreadsheet. I thought I'd figured it all out, but looking back, I can see how mixed up I was—and how much I still had to learn about myself.

Since the social aspects of college still didn't appeal to me and the thought of sharing a dorm with another human sounded terrible, I knew that I would *not* be staying on campus. At the same time, I felt I was ready for more independence and I wanted to try having my own space, so I settled for moving into an apartment nearby campus that would be shared with my best friend, Sadie, and her partner, who would also be attending a college nearby. I thought it would be so much fun becoming more independent and living with people that I knew and felt comfortable with.

So on a hot summer day in July 2016, we all moved in with the help of family and friends. Everything felt fresh, new and exciting. But somewhere deep beneath those feelings was a looming sense of uncertainty and instability. It was like riding a bike without training wheels for the first time—both scary and invigorating. Moving out made me mourn for my childhood, where I would always exist tucked securely under my mother's wing, always safe. I'd had an excuse for my timidity—I was new to this world. It all made me realize that while this was just a practice run of sorts, I would eventually have to do it all on my own, and that overwhelmed me.

Day by day, I became more accustomed to my new life. I developed a routine. I learned to love my space that I had made my own—a minimalist room, a bed with a fluffy, deep purple comforter, pushed against the wall next to a hippy-dippy tapestry with swirls of cool-toned colors to match. I had my own TV in my room, where I faithfully watched one or two episodes of *How I Met Your Mother* on a nightly basis, sometimes accompanied by a plate of cheesy nachos. Ah, cozy.

One thing about me is that I love simplicity and comfort. To this day, I look forward to my nightly couch and reading ritual the way that other people look forward to big events. Winding down is so important to me. It's an essential ending to my days, but at times, it is needed as a break period in the middle of a busier day. It took me a long time to come to terms with this and to accept how necessary those breaks are, but understanding how my brain works helped immensely in getting to this point of acceptance.

You see, an autistic person's brain processes *a lot* more information at rest than does the brain of a neurotypical. Studies have found that approximately 42% more information accounts for this difference.[1] Because of this, we tend to have a hard time filtering out unnecessary stimuli within our surroundings.

For me, one prominent example is how challenging grocery store trips can be for me. Aside from the fluorescent lighting and noise, I am faced with a *huge* variety of products, side by side, covered with colorful labels designed to draw consumers in. When I scan a large array, I tend to take in and process nearly *everything* that I see. Because of this overprocessing of stimuli, it can appear that I'm slower at finding what I need.

The idea that autistics are slow processors is a commonly held assumption, and I guess you could say that it's true. But that's because we are so busy processing *everything* that we can be slower to respond to the "target stimulus," or the main point of focus. I always describe it like this: I have what I refer to as a "running queue" in my head at all times. I can keep up with relatively small amounts of information when it is presented to me at a slow or average pace and when there is not too much competing stimuli in my immediate environment (i.e. background music, side conversations, visual information, or someone loudly chewing corn chips near me, ugh).

But when my brain can't keep up with the information being fed to it, that data starts to build up in a kind of mental queue. For example, during a fast-moving conversation—especially if there are distractions—I might still be processing something that was said a few seconds ago while also trying to hang onto what's currently being said. I don't fully understand the new sentence until I've finished sorting through the last one. Basically, my CPU lags when it's overloaded. And this is exactly why self-care is so important for autistic people—and why my nighttime ritual is so very precious.

Soon after moving and adjusting, things got pretty fun. I looked forward to wing night, when my roommates and I would all get 50-cent wings—I'd always get medium buffalo sauce with blue cheese and carrots. Sadie would always get honey barbecue, then dramatically declare it was spicy—and her partner and I would crack up and tease her about her hopelessly low spice tolerance.

I enjoyed attending college as well. I was finally focusing on courses related to my major and I felt like I was making progress towards a more concrete goal. With each course completion, I was closer to my career.

While I was taking classes, I also worked at a credit union as a teller part-time. I had been working various jobs since I turned 16, both because my parents encouraged it, and because I liked making my own money.

Each job taught me some sort of interesting life skill that I held onto to this day. First, I worked at a southwestern restaurant where I learned to roll a badass burrito. Then, I worked in retail at a clothing store—I still fold my clothes the way I was taught there, and my husband thinks I'm an excellent folder. Next, I started working in banks. Let me tell you, I can count bills really fast and I could probably grab a wad of 20s and magically come extremely close to an exact $1,000. Not sure when I'd ever need to do that again, though.

Working as a teller worked out well for me at the time. I was professional, friendly and efficient. The hardest part of the job was meeting sales goals. My responsibilities included not only processing transactions but also marketing products and services, such as credit card promotions, financial advisors, and member benefits.

I hated doing it because on one hand, I wanted to initiate these conversations using pre-determined scripts that felt smooth and comfortable to me, but on another hand, I wanted to appear authentic. It wasn't easy for me to balance. Being rejected also discouraged me more than it should have (which will make more sense when you get to *The People-Pleasing Paradox* chapter).

I tried to avoid the rejection by neglecting this job responsibility, which then led to more rejection in the form of talks with my manager about not meeting these goals. This started happening periodically, which made me more eager to finish up my degree and get out of there. The pressure was on.

In early 2017, another stressor reared its ugly head when my three-year relationship with my boyfriend quickly began to fall apart. I had been in a long-term relationship with a guy we'll call Tom, who went to the same community college as I did. Between school and downtime, we spent a lot of time together.

I often described Tom as a "nice guy." I mean, he was. He seemed to care deeply for other people and had a strong interest in things like protecting the earth, helping the poor, and building friendships. He went to church and wanted me to go with him. He liked to cook his own food and cared about nutrition. He taught me how to compost. He wasn't into partying or messing around. *How could I possibly be unhappy with this wholesome of a man?* I often thought. Still, something was missing the whole time.

By nature, my emotions run deep. I have always considered myself to be a spiritual person. The natural world isn't just "nature" to me—it feels like something amazing, like a kind of miracle. People, too, are complicated and beautiful in their own messy ways. I don't show this side of me to just anyone, but I'm definitely a romantic at heart. I'm into the idea of fate, have written my fair share of love letters, and have always dreamed of finding someone who feels like home.

That's why we didn't work well together. Although Tom was a genuinely good guy, he wasn't much of a feelings guy. We had discussions about this multiple times when we were together. I needed words of affirmation. I needed depth. He, on the other hand, continued to tell me that he felt incapable of fulfilling these needs for me. *He's just different from me and I need to accept that and stop being so insecure,* I kept thinking. Love is just as much an action as it is a feeling, right?

But when I realized his actions didn't seem to add up either, my feelings for him started plummeting. Over and over, he spoke of marriage, a family, and a quiet life on a little piece of land. It sounded picture-perfect. But when nearly four years had gone by and there was no ring and no plan at all, I couldn't shake the feeling that Tom's "nice guy" endeavors were more important to him than our relationship was. I sensed that we were both a security for each other, a "let's just keep hanging on so that we don't end up lonely one day" kind of deal. And when the hardest chapter of my life arrived and his support was nowhere to be found, the illusion finally broke. That was when I knew: I had to let go. For good.

The Year My Body Said No

This is when I slipped—hard—into my own personal rock bottom. It felt sudden: the shutdown of my functioning, the vanishing of my passion for life, the creeping in of utter fear. Just days before, I'd been approaching all these changes with a kind of fearless optimism. Then, it all shifted.

Just weeks earlier, I was juggling it all: taking 16 credits, completing my assignments on time, working part-time at the bank, managing rent and meals, keeping the apartment clean, and staying connected in my relationships. I would never have guessed that I'd lose all of that—all at once.

I woke up in a panic one day after a serious argument with my boyfriend that ended with both of us realizing our relationship was hanging on by a thread. After that talk, something shifted in my mind that sent me into fight-or-flight mode. The one stable thing I had brought with me alongside all the other life changes was about to be ripped away. I was in a new home, at a new school, in a new city, about to deal with a major breakup.

Suddenly, my whole world felt that much more unfamiliar. I was still trying to relearn where I kept the cups and plates. I couldn't melt blissfully into my bed the same way I used to—the mattress was too new. I still didn't have my schedule down. Yet through all those changes, I still had my partner—our familiar strings of daily conversation, our recycled inside jokes, even our stale, unresolved disagreements we always seemed to circle back to. It all felt like an anchor of safety, until it came loose.

On top of it all, the workload of my courses was weighing on me, keeping me up late at night studying and disrupting my nighttime routine, which at the time I didn't realize was so crucial to my self-care.

Day after day, I woke up filled with more panic and my ability to function was quickly dissipating. I'd open my eyes and immediately feel the room spinning. My heart pounded violently, as if outside my body. I felt like I couldn't breathe, couldn't think, couldn't speak. I'd squeeze my eyes shut, trying to escape the sheer terror I felt—because being awake was so much harder than sleeping. Slowly, after coaxing myself to move and endure the sudden confrontation with reality, some stability would return, and I'd manage to sit up. Bile would rise in my throat, and I'd gag and dry heave. Strangely, it brought a small sense of relief—as if my body were trying to purge all the pressure and fear I'd been holding in.

Eating became a challenge. I constantly had no appetite, and even the thought of putting food into my mouth made me nauseous. I didn't understand why. I *wanted* to eat, but my body said no. And it frightened me, watching myself struggle with something so essential—and watching my will fight, while my flesh rejected everything. I forced myself to have small snacks throughout the day, as much as I could bear, but I still lost a lot of weight over a short period of time.

At first, I tried to go to my classes—tried to push through for as long as I possibly could—but I ended up dissociating and absorbing nothing. When panic attacks hit, I'd flee the room. Outside of the lecture hall, I couldn't focus enough to complete assignments or study. I also tried going to work, hoping that being in a familiar environment with other people might help. Instead, I found myself staring into nothing, fighting the urge to vomit, until I was told I needed to go home—because it was clear I wasn't well enough to be there.

Up until that point, my philosophy was always that "the show must go on." For me, encountering anxiety was just an inevitable part of existence. I was used to pushing myself through situations that felt scary. It had never put my life on hold before, and I never imagined it could have that kind of power over me. But when you keep running a system that's overworked, it eventually combusts. And that's what happened to me.

That was it. My body was forcing me to stop everything, all at once. I dropped all my courses, took a medical leave of absence from work, started anxiety medication, and moved back home to focus on healing. I remember staring at my computer screen, writing emails to my professors as the words blurred through my tears. I remember meeting with my boss and trying to explain something that I didn't even understand myself. I remember the bitterness of that first pill on my tongue, and how I prayed it would silence my swirling thoughts. I felt fully and utterly defeated, ashamed, and embarrassed.

I had no words for what I went through that winter. Was it chronic anxiety? A mental breakdown? And why did it strike so suddenly, so violently? It wasn't until after my diagnosis, many years later, that it actually made sense. My body was reacting to an avalanche of change and pressure: a completely new environment, an overwhelming workload, constant sensory input (seriously, you wouldn't believe how much the apartment's window air units drove me crazy), and far more social interaction than I was used to. It was the perfect storm for an autistic person. And the words I'd been searching for back then? Autistic burnout.

***

A Note On Autistic Burnout

Autistic burnout is a state of physical, emotional, and mental exhaustion that can last anywhere from days to years.[1] It is often accompanied by a loss of previously manageable skills, reduced tolerance for stress, heightened anxiety or depression, increased meltdowns or shutdowns, and even physical illness.[1,2] Burnout is typically caused by prolonged masking, sensory overload, and spending too much time in environments that don't align with an autistic person's needs or neurology.[2]

Many autistic adults who have experienced burnout report that they initially mistook it for depression or another mental health condition.[3] But unlike depression, where common advice might be to socialize, stay busy, or "push through," autistic burnout usually requires the opposite approach. Recovery often involves reducing demands, resting deeply, limiting social interaction when needed, reconnecting with special interests, and getting consistent, restorative sleep.[1,3]

***

I lived the same nightmare every day for at least a month. My mom was my rock during that difficult time, always there reminding me that I could and would conquer it all; She never left my side and always made sure that I ate, rested, and moved. And on top of that, she made me defy my own negative beliefs.

On a given day, I would wake up and do everything I could to get through the harsh transition from sleep to reality. Mornings were always the worst. Even before I opened my eyes, I felt a rush of adrenaline—not the good kind that comes with a long run or a plunge downhill on a rollercoaster, but the kind that sneaks up unwarranted and fabricates an irrational feeling that you're about to be attacked by a bear and not make it out alive. My mom's role was standing between me and my fears, convincing me that there was no bear—and that I was safe.

While there were moments when I thought about letting myself be consumed by darkness, she reminded me that I need to hold on, if even just by starlight. This might have meant sitting up when I felt glued to my bed. Or making myself a cup of chamomile tea when I simply couldn't get my body to settle down.

I remember one particular morning that winter: a snow-storm had recently hit, and everything felt somewhat blurred and dreamy—like I was living inside a snow globe, not really existing, but pretending to. My legs didn't want to move that day. My mind kept ruminating over my condition: how I had gotten so stuck, when—or if—I'd ever feel stable again, and what I'd even do when I got there. I wanted to stay frozen. Somehow, it felt safer that way. It was like I was a volcano holding everything in—heat and pressure swelling beneath the surface, but staying motionless out of fear that one small shift might cause an erup-tion.

But my mom was determined to prove to me that my mind had been lying to me. That morning, she urged me to get up and move, just a little. "Come outside with me," she said. "We're just going to walk up the driveway and back, that's all." I didn't want to. I didn't want to move at all. But she continued to gently coax me until I agreed.

So I bundled up in my winter coat and stepped outside of the house and into the icy cold. My mom and I shuffled back and forth, up and down the driveway, arm in arm. By the time a few minutes had passed, I was laughing at my own stubbornness while my mom joked about how my legs still worked, after all. And by the time we went back inside, I had realized the move-ment actually felt... good. That was the moment I knew that I had to keep challenging myself, in small ways, to keep from sinking.

Slowly, I began to experience moments of calm—moments of happy fading in through the chaos swirling in my mind. Those tiny moments were beautiful. They felt like sun on my skin after the coldest of winters. With the help of prayer, meditation, and the right treatment, things got better and better. I remember thinking that I'd never take my happiness for granted again. I also got in touch with my own inner strength that I never knew I had.

It was then that I put a final end to my rocky, long-term relationship. I hung on a while longer than I should have, clinging to the one thing I had left during those dark days. But upon returning to my reality, I knew Tom was not what I wanted for the rest of my life. But that was only my first realization.

I also came out of it knowing I didn't want to be an accountant. It wasn't that I hated the courses; there were aspects I genuinely enjoyed. But the work didn't fulfill me. It didn't light me up or give me the sense of meaning I was craving. After everything I'd been through with my own mental health, I realized I wanted to do something that felt more personal, something that could make a difference for people like me. I wanted to study psychology, the same major I'd once brushed off as "impractical" and unrealistic.

I've always had an itch to understand people deeply—and even more so, to understand myself. I was constantly analyzing my thoughts, my reactions, and why I often felt so alien around other people. Everything I had gone through only intensified that longing to know *why*. It also instilled in me a deep empathy for people quietly fighting battles inside their own minds.

I wanted to be for them what others had been for me—peace, solace, and most of all, hope. Perhaps that's what pulled me toward the path I was destined to take. I just never would have imagined that I'd have that painful season to thank for it.

So as spring arrived—and with it, my restoration—something changed in me: I decided to free myself. I freed myself from toxic relationships, from pushing myself too hard, and from social expectations that didn't serve me. I started truly accessing who I was on the inside and just doing what made me happy, because happiness, above performance, became my new priority.

Because of this shift, parts of the real "me" began to resurface—pieces I thought I'd left behind as I grew into an adult. I started singing more and making music again. I returned to writing. I started dressing in ways that felt more fun and freeing. I spent more time outside, reconnecting with the earth. Creativity slowly took its place at the center of my life again, because that's what brought me joy and made me feel truly alive.

Am I completely healed? Not even close. To this very day, I continue to wrestle with deep insecurities, emotions that feel too big for my body, and a nagging pressure to be better—because I don't always feel good enough as I am.

But back in the spring of 2017, I loosened the chains that had kept me a prisoner to myself, and I began to let the light in. I felt just a little closer to my authentic self. A little more accepting of my imperfections. And that act of letting go—even just a little—is what shapes a warrior. And even though every war is not won, a strong warrior will keep showing up.

Rivers of Wonder: My Monotropic Mind

My mother always tells me
that I have an addictive personality
because when I find something that I love,
I hold on to it.
I treat it like a flower freshly picked
that I still have time to preserve.
So I put it in a vase
and watch from across the room;
Several feet apart
I let its beauty
wrap around my heart
and enchant me
hour after hour.
And it's only a wildflower,
but I see a rose.
Yes, when something steals me
I drink it in

and expect for it to heal me.
I become intrigued with every detail,
every line.
I write songs and poems about it,
take a picture and frame it
because I don't want to
let myself understand
that things don't always go as planned
and time cannot be frozen
like black and white
will make you think.
With all this time I put
into making my passions
my silver and gold,
forcing flowers to grow in the cold
where they don't want to exist;
With all this time,
I never recognize
the number of petals that have fallen
until the last one
disappears.
And that is what makes
heartbreak so difficult
and failure so frightening
and disappointment so painful.
Because my heart is always
on the edge of a cliff
facing a view so beautiful

that my feet whisper,
"Three more baby steps forward."
I am always prepared to fly,
never to fall.
But there's one thing I've learned
through being such a passionate person
and that is this:
Falling in love with everything
is worth so much more
than the weight of the fall,
because despite the cuts and scrapes
I so often create,
I have felt the magic
that every human being
craves of this life.

I wrote this poem years ago, long before I had any idea that I was autistic. It was written about my intense passions—at the time, what I called my "obsessions." I have always shown an excessive level of attachment to certain people, things, or topics. My family and friends recognized it, and so did I. I just didn't know then that these were my personal special interests.

Having intense, unwavering interests falls under the autism diagnostic criteria, category B: restricted, repetitive patterns of behaviors, interests, or activities, which includes intense, fixated interests.[1] Some stereotypical autistic special interests include math, machines, technology, dinosaurs (or other animal species), trains, coins, plants, archeology, and psychology.

However, anything can be a special interest. The fact that, many times, autistic females have more "socially acceptable" or seemingly normal special interests (such as horses, musical artists, or makeup) is what often causes the atypical intensity of the interest to go unnoticed.[2]

I could go through a long list of special interests that I've had throughout the years, at least as far back as I can remember. In elementary school, I was absolutely obsessed with Hilary Duff. And if you too were a 90s kid, you might be thinking, "Weren't we all?"

Well, sure. To an extent. For me though, this meant trying desperately to mimic her appearance, mannerisms, and singing voice basically as a full-time job. I also plastered my school assignment book with photos of her, talked about her constantly, and researched all the information that I could about her life and interests. I even remember going as far as crying at a sleepover with my best friend in the middle of a passionate monologue about how much I adored her and felt "so inspired" by her. In hindsight, wow. Apologies to my friends for not knowing when to stop.

As I got a little older, I developed intense fixations with other artists in a similar way. All the way from my freshman year of high school to throughout college, I was obsessed with Michael Jackson. At one point, I impulsively purchased a six-foot cardboard cutout of Michael from the *Bad* era. It lived in my room and frequently jump scared my parents and any unlucky guests that happened to walk in during that period of my life.

In high school, my best friend got me a Michael Jackson doll for my birthday, knowing how seriously invested I was (still, one of the most memorable and awesome gifts I've ever received). I even wrote and performed a speech about his life when I was in college. Growing up, my interests were never unknown; I always wore them like a banner. They were more than things I liked; they were extensions of who I was—and ultimately, that never really changed.

Yet, over time, my special interests have since shifted, from people to specialized topics. Appreciating famous artists is fine, but looking back at how much I obsessed over these people makes me cringe every time.

Currently, my special interests are autism, the brain, and psychology—a huge part of why I'm writing this book. I began becoming more interested in autism and neurodivergent brain differences soon after I began my career as a behavior analyst, when I worked primarily with autistic children. Through my studies, I gained a lot of knowledge about human behavior, but I wanted to go deeper. I yearned to know what was happening behind the scenes—in the brain and body—for those autistic children as I engaged with them.

School failed to teach me enough about this perspective, so I taught myself. Naturally, this led me closer to my own self-identification with autism. As my suspicions grew, I started researching more about how autism presents specific to females. From there, my interest intensified even further.

To most people, my obsession with autism and the brain likely looks like work-related enthusiasm. What they don't see is the hours I spend reading, the endless rabbit holes I fall into, or how often I infodump to my endlessly patient husband. What seems like a career interest is something much deeper—a fascination that never ceases.

And as it turns out, I'm in good company. If given the chance, autistic individuals will often choose careers that align with their passions. Your tech-expert friend in IT just may spend even more time geeking out after hours than you know. Of course, this isn't always true; A single trait alone can not define something as complex as autism. But chances are, you know an autistic person already, even though you'd have never expected it.

Most autistics can hyperfocus when engaged in their preferred interests or activities. When we reach this state of hyperfocus, it feels like tunnel vision. We sometimes become unaware of our surroundings and have difficulty with "tuning in" when someone is trying to get our attention.[3] In children, it can look like pointedly ignoring others. Really, they're just completely immersed in what they're doing.

My ability to hyperfocus allows for incredible productivity, effortless information intake without distractions, and a deep sense of joy from doing what I love. This also allows me to be extremely thorough and invested in the work that I do. Because I care, I don't slack.

On the flip side, this can make me even more prone to workplace burnout. While many people may work to solve problems using in-the-moment ideas or trial and error, I don't like to make quick decisions—I prefer to thoroughly research, weigh options, and deeply consider potential outcomes. Having evidence that my decisions are viable options that have worked for others in the past also makes me feel more comfortable executing those ideas.

While this all sounds like good stuff, I have wound up in countless research deep dives that have left me exhausted by the end of the day. And being a bottom-up processor, who tends to focus on small details over the big picture, can slow me down even more. During a project, I might get caught up in choosing PowerPoint color schemes and waste loads of time without even getting to the important content.

Before I knew I was autistic, I labeled myself as a perfectionist, and I hear this a lot from other autistic individuals as well. Monotropism, a term coined in 1992 by autism researcher Dinah Murray, is now used to describe the cognitive style characterized by a narrow focus on a limited range of interests.[4] Broken down, the word translates to "one focus."

This style of thinking explains many key features of autism. For example, autistic children often have difficulties with joint attention, the ability to shift attention or gaze between an object in front of them and another individual who is engaging with that same object. A neurotypical child will stack blocks to create a tall tower, then look up at a nearby adult for their reaction. The adult then might attempt to join in the play by driving a toy dump truck into their own tower, knocking it over. The neurotypical child would watch the tower tumble down, then look up and share laughs or an expression of surprise with their adult play partner.

In contrast, an autistic child may focus intently on the objects the entire time, directing smiles, frustrations, and determination straight to the objects without shifting attention to nearby play partners.

Monotropism also explains why autistic individuals often struggle with transitions—their focus on the activity at hand may be so strongly fixed that they require other tools such as verbal warnings, timers, or organized schedules in order to ease the move away from one activity and onto another. Besides these examples, monotropic individuals tend to:

- Feel highly frustrated when interrupted during activities or conversations

- Find multitasking difficult and mentally draining

- Get caught in thought loops, repeatedly thinking about or talking about the same thing over and over

- Forget or overlook tasks that don't personally interest them

- Zone out during conversations that don't center on their personal interests

- Struggle with decision making, especially when overwhelmed with multiple choices

- Startle easily at sudden noises or unexpected changes

- Engage in special interests as a way to calm or self-soothe

- Prefer individual projects to working with a group

- Struggle to follow group discussions when multiple people are speaking at once

- Have trouble letting go of a problem until it feels resolved

To get an idea of how monotropic you may be, I recommend taking the Monotropism Questionnaire, a screening tool developed in 2023 that measures an individual's "monotropism score" against both the neurotypical and autistic standards. Researchers have found that a high score is predictive of autism and correlates with other reliable autism screening tools, such as RAADS-R and AQ.

My monotropic thinking style is apparent in many of my behaviors, spanning from childhood to now. As a little girl, I was very good at independent play and could keep focused attention on an activity for long periods of time. I was—and still am—meticulous with almost everything I do, unless it's something that doesn't interest me.

I can recall a very specific moment in preschool when I was *so* intently focused that I wet my pants. I was working on a project where I had to stick red and green apple stickers onto a paper tree in specific spots. I realized partway through that I *really* had to pee, but I was determined to finish without interruption. I was also very particular about neatness, so a rushed, sloppy job wasn't an option.

I held it in until I had finished my project, then got up to ask the teachers if I could use the bathroom. But they were in the middle of a conversation at the time and didn't notice me standing there right away. Being the timid girl that I was, I didn't want to interrupt, so I waited. But I was just a little too late—the accident happened. A teacher rushed me to the bathroom while I melted with embarrassment. I hadn't had bathroom accidents in a long time, so I was mortified—likely the reason why this memory stuck with me so vividly.

Looking back, this is such a clear example of my ability to hyperfocus. I was so engrossed in the task at hand that even my bodily needs took a back seat.

Fast forward to elementary school, where my family nickname of "the human sewing machine" was first dubbed. Backstory: my fifth-grade teacher was an older lady with a deep love for quilting. She shared her passion with the class by showing off her personal projects, having us each contribute a square to a classroom quilt, and even launching her own summer quilting camp for anyone interested. I liked the idea and decided to give it a try that summer—and I won't lie, I was good.

While many autistics struggle with fine motor skills, others seem to be exceptional in this area, proven by savants who have extraordinary abilities in things like drawing, painting, or playing musical instruments. I am not a savant by any means, but my fine motor skills have always been strong. Paired with a detail-oriented mind and a dash of perfectionism, this has definitely benefited me in some areas.

"Her stitches look like they were done by a sewing machine," my teacher told my mother as she shared my completed quilting camp project. My mom has held onto it all these years, and when I finally saw it again, I couldn't believe it myself. Each stitch was freakishly uniform—so precise and evenly spaced that you'd think a machine made it, not a ten-year-old with a needle and thread.

Middle school through high school was when I really began identifying my unique interests—and entered a monotropic state where nothing else seemed to matter to me. I spent most days lost in daydreams, sitting behind my desk at school writing poetry and prose, paying no mind to what I was supposed to be focused on. I felt I wanted to create. And that was when I found that my own imaginative world was more fulfilling than the real one.

My teachers either thought I was dumb or just lazy. Getting called on unexpectedly would make me jolt back into reality with no idea what was just being discussed or what question I was supposed to be answering. Sometimes I'd look up in silence, dumbfounded. Other times, I'd frantically flip through pages, sweating, eyes darting around the room searching for any kind of context that might help me figure out what I was supposed to say.

Somehow, I managed high school with mostly good grades. My great memory likely helped to compensate for my lack of attention during class. My strategy? I would drift off into my own mental universe during class, teach myself the material later (because reading the textbook has always made more sense to me than relying on lectures anyway), and cram information into my brain in as short an amount of time as possible before being tested on it.

I imagine that if I had put in more effort, I would have been a straight-A student. But that just wasn't what I cared about at the time. College, though, was my time to shine—once I was able to focus on my area of interest.

Like I mentioned before, I thought I wanted to be an accountant because I saw it as the most logical career choice. And I gave it a fair shot. I studied hard, stayed on top of my assignments, and got good grades. Yet the entire time, something just didn't feel quite right. I didn't feel confident sitting in rooms full of people who seemed so enthused by business and finance. It somehow felt unnatural—because for me, the passion just wasn't there.

I kept trying to force this idea into my head: that my career could be separate from my passion—that a job didn't need to be fun, just practical. And sure, that works for some people. But could I really spend 40+ hours a week doing something I thought was just okay?

After burning out in 2017, my priorities shifted. I started caring more about my happiness than about making the "logical" choice. I returned to school—and to myself—as a psychology major. I left accounting behind. I left my ex-boyfriend behind. And I left behind the belief that I had to keep pushing myself to do things that didn't serve my soul.

My original plan was to become a therapist. I wanted to help people who struggled with mental health, like I did. My battle with anxiety and depression instilled in me a deep empathy for others who knew that kind of pain.

So I jumped back into courses with a fresh sense of wonder and excitement for what the future might hold. Almost immediately, I felt like I was in the right place. The people around me seemed more like-minded, and for the first time in a long time, I didn't feel nearly as awkward interacting with classmates. Learning about the human mind was, and still is, absolutely exhilarating to me.

Towards the end of my program, I was required to do a capstone course that included an internship experience. I applied to several, not set on anything specific. I ended up getting accepted to an internship where I would work with children at an after-school program. To be a part of the program, the child had to have some sort of mental health diagnosis or developmental disability.

The program combined psychoeducation, therapeutic activities, and elements of applied behavior analysis (ABA)—a therapy commonly recommended for children with autism. At that point, I had taken an introductory course in behavior analysis, but I hadn't yet seen what it looked like in real-world practice. I also felt strongly that I didn't want to work with children. "I'm not big on kids," I'd casually tell people. But when it came to choosing an internship, I wasn't in a position to be picky. I took what was available and figured it might be fun—or at the very least, informative.

The program divided the kids into three different classrooms: young children, adolescents, and those with autism. When I had a choice, I'd always ask to be with the little ones. Teenagers were intimidating, and, ironically enough, I had no particular interest in working with autistic kids either.

I started the internship with the mindset that it was just another step towards finishing my degree. I left with a full heart and a newfound love for little people. And as a girl with a one-track mind, once passion blooms, it doesn't die easily. I didn't know it yet, but that spark had already started pulling me in a new direction from what I'd planned—and it became a big part of what led me down the path I ended up taking later on.

Does my obsessive, monotropic brain drive me a little crazy sometimes? Absolutely. There are plenty of moments when I wish I could flip a switch, shut it off, and leave that narrow world inside my head for another day. But all in all, it's also what's gotten me where I am today. And the joy, the drive, the zest for learning, and all the fruit it bears is so much greater what makes it hard.

The Autistic Analyst: Reconciling Practice with Lived Experience

The end of my internship was far more bittersweet than I expected. Over just a few short months, my heart began to swell with a new and unexpected love for working with children. This stirring led me to change my mind, yet again, about what I wanted to do.

So after graduating, I decided to pursue a career in behavior science instead of becoming a therapist, as I had originally planned. While researching my options, I came across the role of a behavior analyst and found it intriguing. A behavior analyst is a professional who uses the science of learning and behavior to help individuals learn important life skills as well as reduce harmful or inappropriate behaviors, using a therapy called Applied Behavior Analysis (ABA).

I was drawn to the combination of understanding human behavior through a scientific lens while also working closely with individuals to support meaningful change. The field emphasizes evidence-based practice and uses data to guide decision-making, which really appealed to my analytical side. I ended up pursuing this career—but it wasn't until years later that I learned many in the autistic community have serious concerns about the use of ABA, particularly regarding the ethics of how it's been used historically for autistic individuals.

ABA is often referred to as the "gold standard" therapy for improving outcomes in autistic children. So why is it so controversial? To understand the debate, it helps to start with the basics of human behavior.

Our behavior is largely influenced by three things: motivation, reinforcement, and punishment. In this context, punishment doesn't mean discipline—it refers to *any* experience that makes us less likely to repeat a behavior. For example, if your boss criticizes an idea you share in a meeting, you may feel less inclined to speak up next time. That comment functioned as a punisher.

Reinforcement, on the other hand, is what increases the likelihood of repeating a behavior in the future. Though many tend to think of it strictly as a reward—like giving a child a lollipop for cleaning up—we come in contact with reinforcement all day long. You brush your teeth to avoid cavities (negative reinforcement), or smile at a stranger because you once got a smile in return (positive reinforcement). But if certain social behaviors, like eye contact or smiling, feel uncomfortable or effortful for someone, they may naturally avoid them. Reinforcement is personal, and behavior is shaped by what feels rewarding for each individual.

Motivation is always connected to reinforcement and punishment—it controls the likelihood of a behavior happening based on how valuable the outcome is in that moment. Some basic examples: if you're short on money, you're more likely to work overtime (the behavior) in order to earn money (the reinforcer). Similarly, if you've just run a marathon, water becomes more reinforcing because it's more valuable when you're thirsty than when you're not.

Now, let's get to the controversy. As behavior scientists who work directly with complex human beings, just having this sort of knowledge brings both responsibility and risk. Knowing how to shape new behaviors or stop existing ones is not something to be taken lightly. At the same time, when applied ethically and compassionately, we can use ABA as a powerful learning tool to impart meaningful skills and support long-term independence.

The truth of the matter is that ABA has the capacity to be both harmful and helpful. While many families report it as the most effective therapy for their autistic children, the approach also carries a deeply troubling history. Developed in the 1960s, ABA is still a relatively new intervention—and many autistic adults who experienced it in childhood are now speaking out about the long-term harm they endured. Accounts from the autistic community include being forced to make eye contact in exchange for rewards, being subjected to electric shock as a form of punishment, and spending up to eight hours a day doing repetitive table work as very young children.

In reading about autism, from research to advocacy pieces to personal reflections, I've seen widespread criticism of ABA. Many of these concerns are valid, and even those who haven't experienced the therapy firsthand speak out to educate and protect others. I don't blame them. But as an autistic behavior analyst, I also feel a responsibility to shed light on what compassionate, neurodiversity-affirming ABA looks like today—because it does exist. Just like with any profession, from doctors to therapists, the quality and approach of the provider matters. And in ABA, it can make all the difference.

First, let's discuss some ways in which ABA has evolved from its beginning in the 60s:

- The Behavior Analyst Certification Board (BACB) developed a comprehensive Code of Ethics in 2001 to enforce ethical practices, and it continues to be regularly updated. This code allows anyone to report harmful practices to the Board, which can result in a BCBA's (Board Certified Behavior Analyst) certification being suspended or permanently revoked, depending on the severity of the case.[1]

- The use of Positive Behavior Support (PBS) emerged in the 1980s, shifting the focus from punishment-based procedures to reinforcement-based strategies. Today, it is considered best practice to avoid using punishment altogether. Research has also shown that reinforcement is generally more effective for long-term behavior change than punishment.[2]

- Electric shock therapy has been disowned and condemned by virtually all ABA providers in the U.S. Only one known center continues to use this practice, and many professionals in the field—along with autistic advocates—are actively fighting to end it entirely.[3]

- Many ABA professionals are now listening to autistic adults and allowing their voices to shape how therapy is delivered. For instance, after hearing from autistic individuals who were taught to make eye contact and described it as deeply uncomfortable—even physically painful—practitioners now avoid eye contact goals. Instead, they offer alternative ways for individuals to acknowledge when someone is speaking to them.[4]

- In the early 2000s, the concept of trauma-informed care became more widely known. High-quality ABA providers now incorporate this approach by assuming trauma may have impacted a learner's life and avoiding forceful or invasive interventions that could trigger a trauma response.[5]

- Play-based models are now widely used in early intervention. We understand that children learn best through play—not through rigid, repetitive tablework. Old-school ABA often relied on flashcards, extended sessions, and minimal breaks during hours of intensive therapy. But kids were never meant to sit at a desk for eight hours a day without autonomy or freedom—there is nothing okay about that. Today, we flip the model: instead of inserting bits of play into therapy, we insert bite-sized pieces of therapy into play. This creates a more positive, trusting relationship between the therapist and learner. We want kids to feel safe with us—and to actually want to come to therapy![6]

Dignity, compassion, and respect are now core principles within the field. Seeing our learners as humans with the same rights that we all have is part of the BACB Code of Ethics. Some ways that I personally practice this principle are by teaching self-advocacy, allowing learners to opt out of participating in therapy, teaching learners to be as independent as they can be, and recognizing that the goal of treatment is not to create a neurotypical human, but to teach skills that actually matter. (So no—it's not true that all ABA practitioners want to stop your kids from flapping their hands.)[1]

Although accounting wasn't my destiny, my affinity for numbers remains. Seeing a graph confirming a child's consistent skill acquisition is reassuring. And if a particular intervention isn't working, I can use data to quickly pick up on that and know it's time to try something different. Along with objective data, it's also important to have discussions with families and consider how they're feeling about therapy. I might ask if parents are noticing positive changes, if their children seem happy in therapy, if anything makes them uncomfortable, and whether they feel we're focusing on the most important goals for their children.

So, this is my personal behind-the-scenes perspective on ABA, as part practitioner, part neurodivergent insider. I don't write to deny its dark history or any real, lived experiences had by autistics today. I also don't claim that every clinic that exists today has completely moved away from the old-school ABA model. But I do want to set the record straight since it seems that many people are still being fed stale information—claims that *all* ABA is bad and assumptions that our field has not made any effort to grow since the 60s. My hope is that as research progresses and more autistics speak out about their inner experiences, we will grow more and more. As both an autistic person and a behavior analyst, I feel that I have a deep responsibility—one where I feel called to both protect my community and to speak honestly about what I believe to be a life-changing form of therapy, given the right team.

***

High-Quality ABA Green Flags

When assessing the quality of an ABA provider, ask the following questions:

1. Does the provider value and/or teach consent and as-

sent?

2. Does the provider involve caregivers in the goal-selection process, as well as important members of the care team?

3. Does the provider select meaningful goals, rather than goals like suppressing stims or making a child appear more neurotypical?

4. Does the provider adjust interventions in a timely fashion when they notice that something isn't working?

5. Does the provider encourage all types of play, rather than insisting on functional play (i.e., playing with toys as they were intended to be used)?

6. Does the provider incorporate your child's personal interests into learning opportunities? Does your child seem happy to have therapy?

7. Does the provider avoid excessive use of token systems or food as rewards?

8. Does the provider take thorough time to assess and understand the "why" behind a concerning behavior before jumping into treatment?

9. Does the provider acknowledge sensory needs and emotional expression?

10. Does the provider value self-advocacy and the ability to choose reasonable alternatives over compliance?

If you can answer "yes" to all of these, chances are you've found a potential fit for your loved one. These are all signs that point to therapy being neurodiversity-affirming and far from outdated methods.

The most important piece of advice I'd give to someone seeking ABA for a loved one is to view your BCBA as both a team member and a coach. You, as a parent or caregiver, are your child's biggest advocate! Ask loads of questions. Tell us what makes you uncomfortable. Be open. And most of all... call out the crap. We want to do better, and that's the only way we will.

A Soft Landing

I didn't expect to meet my person right after feeling like my life had fallen apart, but somehow, along came the man who would love me fully, despite all my little quirks, and all my big emotions. Shortly after my "rock bottom" experience and finally returning to normal functioning, I met Matthew. I had decided to try out online dating, but my first attempt resulted in the wrong guy, emotional manipulation, and a string of regrets. I left after a few months without looking back, but I dragged some more hurt and distrust along with me. At that point, all I wanted was to be done with wasting my time on men who didn't matter enough. I was over it.

Around that time, I found myself crying in the car one day, thinking about all those failed relationships, when I looked up and saw a church sign that said something rather cliché about praying and bringing everything to God. For some reason, I felt the need to break down and do it—right then and there. I prayed and told God that I no longer wanted to waste my time. With swollen eyes and vision clouded by tears, I uttered, "Don't allow me to get involved in another relationship unless it's the one."

A week or so later, I hopped back onto the online dating app, this time very cautiously, and with very low expectations. I swiped around a bit, wondered if I should just delete the app and let it go for a while, and then decided that I needed to at least say hello to this dude who kept repeatedly popping up as a suggestion. The app had the nerve to make the bold claim that we were "99% compatible." I skimmed over his profile and saw that he liked both *How I Met Your Mother* and sushi, two really great things. I sent him a quick message remarking about his great taste, and that was that.

At some point, we exchanged numbers and began talking every day. Then, he asked me to meet him for coffee. I remember telling my best friend, Sadie, and roommate at the time, "I'm meeting this guy for coffee. I'm not going to agree to see him again unless we have some crazy connection and things go absolutely amazing." I was convinced at the time that she thought I was crazy and desperate, based on the events of the past few months.

Well, I came back from the date embarrassed to say that things *had* gone absolutely amazing and that there *was* a weird connection between us. *She is not going to believe me. I mean, what are the odds that this is the one?* I thought. Despite all of my efforts to take things slow, things progressed very quickly from that point on. And by things, I mean emotional connection sorts of things—the good stuff. I'm pretty sure that by two weeks in, we had made a bucket list of things to do together over the summer. Looking back, it seems extremely weird. Yet at the time, it somehow felt completely natural. It was almost as if we'd already known each other and were just reconnecting, rather than meeting for the first time. Matthew felt like home to me—he was an immediate safe person, and I never really felt the need to hide much of myself from him.

Still, there were things that he learned about me as time went on. He learned that I get really weird and uncomfortable at parties, that I don't prefer much to travel, and that I am really, really emotional and will cry when I am happy, sad, mad, overwhelmed, and just about everything in between.

He once took me to a house party hosted by a few of his casual friends, and when we left, I cried and admitted I hated it. I worried I had misread him—that he wasn't the mellow guy I thought he was, and that he went to parties all the time.

"I'm afraid this might not work out," I said, panicking, because I liked him so much. He reassured me that he wasn't really into those kinds of parties either and didn't go often—but as a single guy living alone, he liked having people around. So he'd show up more to maintain friendships than out of a love for the party scene. Even that night, he'd been one of the quieter ones.

I was shocked by the nurturing response he gave me, and I knew he was being honest. But I was so used to past boyfriends telling me I wasn't fun or spontaneous enough—always, subtly, trying to change me and disguising it as something that would be good for me.

As I got to know Matthew more and more, I learned that he is, by nature, very levelheaded and calm. Yes, there is another side of him that craves adrenaline and has led him to hobbies like car racing and rock climbing, to get his fill. Yet, he and I go together quite close to perfectly. Sometimes I ask myself why that is. How did I wind up in such harmony with a neurotypical man? While Matt doesn't experience life in exactly the same way that I do, the way that our lives are structured together allows for us to both thrive in our own ways.

For example, Matt also enjoys routines and a habitual sort of everyday lifestyle. He just doesn't cry when it gets thrown off, like I do. Therefore, our day-to-day is structured and planned for the most part. Matt will review his week ahead with me. We'll sit down periodically and put together lists and plans for the upcoming months. We typically have a flexible weekend routine too—and if that changes, I know about it in advance. Not to mention I love that he's okay with cycling through the same three restaurants for takeout most of the time without getting tired of them!

It's pretty well known that autistic children oftentimes prefer parallel play over interactive play, meaning they like to do things *alongside* peers rather than always directly interact with them. Well, that's me. I also love parallel play, or should I say parallel hobbying? Doing hobbies together but separately? You get the point. For us, this usually looks like Matt on one side of the couch gaming and myself on the other side, either reading, writing, or playing my own game on my Nintendo Switch.

Especially after having kids (spoiler: we get married and have kids!), my "me time" is precious and frankly, important to my mental health. It helps me to de-stress and recharge. I appreciate the quiet time that I have to do my own thing, but even more so, I appreciate being in the company of my favorite person without obligation to do any one thing in particular. Since we do have our own interests that matter a lot to each of us, we started delegating one night a week to just being together—a mid-week date night (but in the house, while our kids are sleeping). It could be as simple as a movie and fresh-baked cookies, but it gives us something new to look forward to.

Perhaps what I appreciate the most about Matt is the way that he accepts me and acknowledges my feelings, even when my feelings might not make sense to anyone but me. Frankly, it's something that I'm not used to. I feel like I've been told over and over again throughout my life that unpleasant feelings were meant to be pushed away—that happiness should be my baseline. But that is so unrealistic, and it's especially unrealistic for someone like me, who experiences so many emotions so deeply. We all want to be happy. We all want to be able to magically tolerate what makes us feel uncomfortable. But sometimes what we need is for someone to just sit with us and simply love us for exactly who we are. For me, that someone is him. In a world that often asked me to shrink or adjust, he made space for me to just be—and that has changed everything.

No Filter: The Cost of Feeling Everything

Being autistic means experiencing everything at a high intensity. While my world often feels sharp, loud, and all-consuming, I've also found that this kind of vivid perception can also be quite beautiful. My autism causes layers of sounds to feel overwhelming and certain textures to make my skin crawl in disgust, but it also creates rich, movie-scene-like memories and a capacity to feel even the simplest joy in full color. It's a blessing and a curse—a mind that seesaws from extreme to extreme.

Every autistic person experiences sensory challenges differently. Some are more hypersensitive, meaning they experience heightened responses to environmental stimuli. Others are hyposensitive, experiencing reduced sensitivity. Many of us experience both, depending on the situation. Changes in how I process the world around me can depend on several factors. For instance, I've noticed that when I'm tired or have had an exceptionally busy day, my sensitivity to sound and touch increases significantly. On the flip side, I can tolerate these same stimuli much better after a calm, quiet day—especially one with minimal social interaction and sensory input.

The sensory system as a whole includes several categories of input. You're probably already familiar with the five basic senses: sight, hearing, smell, taste, and touch. But there are three additional senses—vestibular, proprioceptive, and interoceptive—that play an equally important role in how we interpret and interact with the world.[1] While everyone processes sensory input differently, autistic people often experience it at much more intense extremes. Here's a brief look at how that can show up:

Hypersensitivity:

- Preference for dim lighting due to light sensitivity

- Focus on details rather than the big picture

- Fragmented or distorted visual processing

- Difficulty filtering sounds; background noise can be overwhelming

- Heightened awareness of subtle sounds (like buzzing electricity)

- Sensitivity to smells, often disliking strong fragrances

- Preference for bland foods over strong or spicy flavors

- Aversion to grooming tasks due to tactile sensitivity

- Preference for deep pressure; aversion to light touch

- Discomfort with certain fabrics, tags, or seams

Hyposensitivity:

- Poor depth perception; may appear clumsy

- Difficulty noticing certain sounds

- Preference for loud music or noisy environments

- Weakened sense of smell or need to lick objects

- Preference for strong, spicy, or sour flavors

- Tendency to mouth or chew on objects

- High pain tolerance

- Craving deep pressure or use of weighted blankets

- Soothing through touching specific textures like putty or plushie

For me, sensory differences show up mostly as heightened sensitivity to sound and touch, though this can vary from day to day. My biggest trigger is layered sounds, multiple noises happening simultaneously. People tend to assume that autistics are sensitive only to loud noises. This can be true for some of us, but for others, it's less about volume and more about the complexity of sound. I can enjoy a concert (if it's music I really love), but driving in light rain with the radio on and my toddler chatting in the back seat? Overload. I lose focus. My system gets overwhelmed.

Other times, it's a single, persistent sound at just the wrong frequency that sets me off. Usually, these are sounds that other people just don't notice or can easily ignore. My husband knows that I am notorious for turning off the bathroom fan too quickly after a shower or cooking without the oven fan running. I once stayed in a motel with window air units and couldn't sleep because of the noise. They're not just "annoying"—they're invasive, triggering an urgent need to escape.

So how does sensory overload feel? For me, it's like standing on the edge of a meltdown. Sometimes it feels like anxiety coursing through my body; other times, it hits as a wave of raw irritability. Put simply, overstimulation can make me mean, which sucks. The longer I'm exposed to sensory triggers, the more pressure I feel building inside—like a balloon stretching tighter and tighter, ready to burst. There's a restless, pent-up energy, paired with an irrational kind of frustration that makes me scared to open my mouth—because if I speak, I might explode. And when I can't remove myself to reset or regulate, I often shut down instead, going quiet and distant just to cope.

Strangely, it took me *years* to recognize these feelings for what they were—sensory overload. I used to feel irritable or anxious, seemingly out of nowhere, and not know why. Because I didn't make the connection between my internal feelings and my external environment, I never knew how to cope. I didn't remove myself, make accommodations, or even pause and observe what was happening. For a long time, I figured my mood swings were just random, and all I could do was wait them out.

In the time leading up to my official autism diagnosis, I began observing my feelings and behaviors much more closely, trying to determine whether autism was truly a fitting explanation based on the diagnostic criteria. It didn't take long to spot patterns that confirmed my "mystery" distress wasn't so arbitrary after all.

For example, when I had panic attacks, they would often happen in places like the mall, restaurants, and church worship services. What do all these things have in common? Lots of noise, bright lights, or a combination of the two.

I started noticing smaller patterns too—like how irritable I felt during and after long car rides when my husband played music the entire time, especially songs heavy in treble. I also realized how much calmer I felt shopping at Walmart during their sensory-friendly hours, and how quickly that calm vanished when the lights and volume returned to normal. Suddenly, I felt the need to book it. Shopping trip over!

Eventually, I got myself a pair of active noise canceling headphones. What an incredible invention. Having them on hand for especially challenging situations has had a huge impact, helping me navigate those moments with much more ease. Even more importantly, I've learned to notice when I need a break—and to respond with compassion instead of pushing through.

The Three Extra Senses

Beyond the basic five senses are three lesser-known but equally important types of sensory input: vestibular, proprioceptive, and interoceptive.

The vestibular system is responsible for our sense of balance. An underactive vestibular system may result in a strong craving for movement such as rocking, spinning or swinging, which can all help to fulfill this need. On the reverse side, an overactive vestibular system can lead to difficulties controlling movement during active games like sports. Frequent car sickness can also occur because of this.

Proprioception, another part of our complex sensory system, refers to body awareness. Individuals with hyposensitive proprioception can easily get labeled as clumsy, because they may have less of a sense of where their bodies are in space and in relation to objects. They may bump into things often or stand too close to others, showing less of an awareness of personal space. If instead, they have an hypersensitive proprioceptive system, they may show deficits in fine motor skills, like manipulating buttons, writing utensils, or other small objects.

Lastly, interoception is responsible for allowing us to feel and recognize our bodies' signals—signals such as hunger, thirst, the urge to use the bathroom, temperature changes, and even emotions. This important sense can also be different in individuals with autism or sensory processing disorder (SPD). Some individuals barely register these sensations, while others feel them more intensely than most.[1] This helps explain why some autistic people have an unusually high or low pain tolerance.

Interoception helps us to sense pain and other sensations, like those previously listed. Some autistics notice the feeling of a full bladder more strongly than neurotypicals do, resulting in frequent bathroom usage. Others wait until the last minute because of poor interoception. The same thing can happen with hunger and thirst. People with under-responsive interoception may even mix up body signals. They might feel that something is "not quite right" in their body but struggle to pinpoint whether it's hunger, thirst, sadness, or simply the need to use the bathroom.

The one area where my sense of interoception affects me most significantly is emotional regulation. As mentioned earlier, this system includes the category of emotional intelligence, which also involves the ability to regulate emotions.

Emotional regulation has always been an enormous challenge for me. Until I found out that I was autistic, I often wondered why I was so prone to stress and why strong emotions always seemed to overtake me—to the point of being unable to get myself back to a state of equilibrium, of balanced calm.

I experience emotions at extremely high intensities. This means that when I am sad, it feels like the world is ending. And when I am angry, I feel like I'm burning up from the inside.

It also means that when I love, I love hard. When I see beauty, it brings me to tears. And when I am happy, my body becomes filled with joy that makes me want to jump, dance, and bask in the fact that I am simply alive.

It can be hard to pick apart these emotions. When I feel a feeling, it never seems subtle or gradual. Sometimes, I don't realize that I am upset until I am welling with rage or feeling warm tears streaming down my cheeks.

Because I experience emotions to such a high degree, it seems impossible to intentionally try to control them. I can't usually stop myself from crying when I feel strongly, even after time has passed by and I should be able to move on. I can't let something roll off my back when it stirs a passion in me. I can't easily decide to respond to anxiety in a healthy or logical way.

This neurological difference, combined with the hormonal shifts that came with being a female, created the perfect storm any time I experienced fluctuations—especially during my menstrual cycle. I remember that shortly after getting my first period as a teen, my moods took a wild turn. I'd have intense outbursts that rivaled toddler tantrums. I often joke that I transformed into a complete nightmare overnight—like I turned 13 and woke up a monster the next day.

My parents assumed I needed more discipline, which made sense given how I sometimes treated them. But what I really needed was help with managing my big emotions—a toolbox for emotional regulation.

And honestly, I'd argue that's something every child deserves. Teaching and practicing emotional intelligence can, and should, begin as early as the toddler years. At the end of this chapter, I'll share a few simple ways to start.

Thankfully, as our understanding of the brain and emotions grows—and as mental health becomes a more open conversation—each generation seems to do a little better than the last. Many millennial parents I know take emotional development seriously, likely because so many of us had to learn how to handle big feelings without much support ourselves. Gone are the days of, "Stop crying or I'll give you something to cry about." We may not have it all figured out, but the good news is: we're learning right alongside our kids.

My parents did the best that they could with what they knew. But like most adults back then, they simply didn't have the language or understanding that we now have around neurodivergence, emotions, and regulation.

The good news is that as a generation, we are shifting the focus from making kids just behave to making them emotionally aware and regulated—which naturally results in happier kids who have a more cooperative relationship with adults rather than one of blind submission.

As both an autistic adult and a parent myself, I am given the honor of both relearning how to manage my emotions while actively giving my kids the tools that I didn't have back then.

I'm not a perfect parent. I still lose my patience. I get completely overwhelmed. I don't always know how to respond. But I'm learning that even when I find myself in the trenches of dysregulation, the most important thing that I can do is model something that is more important than perfection: self-forgiveness—and the gentle return to myself, no matter how messy the path was getting there.

***

Helping Yourself

- **Know your triggers.** Take some time for self observation in order to better understand your personal sensory needs. How do you respond to specific environmental conditions? What precursor feelings or behaviors do you notice before you find yourself in full sensory overload? Write down your triggers along any other observations so that you can catch sensory challenges and employ effective coping strategies at the first signs.

- **Create a toolbox.** This includes accommodations and coping strategies. Accommodations may include carrying noise-canceling headphones or earbuds, fidget items, or comfort items. Coping strategies might mean taking a break in a quiet room, focusing on your breath, or engaging in movement that makes your body feel good.

- **Communicate your needs.** It can be difficult to be open with others about how you are feeling. It's especially hard for those of us who are used to pushing through and trying our best to blend in. If this is you, try starting with one "safe person"—a spouse, friend, or family member that you feel comfortable with. Discuss ways that this person can be helpful during moments of sensory overload, including what they should not do. For example, some people need a giant, deep pressure hug while others need plenty of space. Some people enjoy talking through things while others feel like they can't get words out when overstimulated. Making these details known while you are calm can prevent misunderstandings and accidental outbursts in the moment.

Helping Your Autistic Loved One

- **Ask how you can help.** Get to know your loved one's personal triggers and what helps them during times of overstimulation. For example, hugs or no hugs? Talking or no talking? What items can be offered to make things easier? It's different for everyone, so try to be aware of likes and dislikes. *Establish this when the autistic person is calm—not when they are already in the middle of sensory overload.*

- **Willingly make accommodations.** Your perspective and attitude about providing accommodations is arguably more important than the action of doing so, in this case. Autistic individuals are often used to enduring uncomfortable things for the sake of everyone else's comfort. But what if the switch was flipped? There are probably more people in the world who enjoy loud music and a lively social circle than those who are opposite, but that doesn't make one single neurotype "right." Lovingly embracing other people's differences and making simple accommodations for them rather than expecting them to "push through" is another great step towards normalizing diverse brains.

- **Understand that sensory needs change all the time.** Responding to someone in distress by saying, "But you handled this okay before," is not helpful. As I've described earlier in the chapter, our sensory system varies all the time based on a number of factors. Besides, you don't need to understand someone's "why" in order to show compassion. Aside from these physiological changes, there may be other reasons someone starts showing signs of struggle when they haven't before, such as: (1) they may be working on unmasking and have decided to stop camouflaging their differences, (2) they may be in a state of burnout and no longer able to mask or suppress difficulties, even if they once could, or (3) literally any other reason. Just be kind.

***

Teaching Children Emotional Intelligence

The ability to recognize, label, and regulate emotions has been shown to strengthen important life skills such as empathy, social competence, and resilience.[2] Here are a few simple ways to start teaching young children about their big feelings:

- **Help them to identify and label emotions.** When big feelings arise, a part of our brain called the amygdala is activated, which sends the body into fight-or-flight mode. This means that the heart rate increases, muscles get tense, and adrenaline is released into the bloodstream.[2] If you were about to be attacked by a wild animal, this is the sort of response that you would experience. Another part of the brain, the prefrontal cortex, counteracts the amygdala's activity by activating rationalization and logical thinking.[2] And guess what? Children's prefrontal cortices are extraordinarily underdeveloped![2] This is why having a sandwich cut into triangles instead of squares can sometimes seem so detrimental to little brains. They can't logic their way out of the new and uncomfortable situation. When I am tempted to call out the ridiculousness of my tiny 3-year old son, this is what I try to remember. The good news is that there are ways to intentionally work on developing emotional regulation. Research has found that by simply labeling our emotions as we experience them, we activate the prefrontal cortex (the center for rational-ization) as well as slow down activity in the amygdala (which controls fight-or-flight).[3] So when our children are expressing their feelings through yells, cries, or ag-gression, help them label their inner experience to the best of your ability.

- **Teach coping strategies.** Model appropriate ways to handle distress, like taking deep breaths, counting to 10, stomping, or squeezing a stress ball. There are so many more out there, too. We can't always expect our littles to start using these skills right away, especially not in the middle of an emotional meltdown or tantrum, so be sure to provide practice during calm moments.

- **Give choices.** When big feelings arise, we often feel out of control—and this is especially true for children. By providing some autonomy when it comes to a calm down routine, we are utilizing *shared control* or *limited control.* When kids have a sense of agency, they're more likely to participate willingly and build self-regulation skills in the process.

An example of putting these techniques together may look like this: "I can see that you are feeling ___ because ___. Do you want to take a deep breath or count with me?" Modify according to age and cognitive ability, keeping sentences short and simple for young toddlers and elaborating a bit more for older children.

Probably Don't Throw Me a Surprise Party

Change has always been difficult for me, especially the kind that arrives suddenly, without warning. My routines are more than just preferences—they're what hold my days together, bringing a sense of calm and familiarity to a world that can sometimes feel like too much. In fact, I'd say my deep attachment to sameness is one of my most defining autistic traits. When that sense of order is disrupted, even in small ways, I can quickly become dysregulated. Some examples of when this happens include:

- When I have an appointment or event that is different from my typical daily routine (like a mid-day dentist appointment)

- When parts of my environment change dramatically (for example, spending extended time away from my home and having to bathe and sleep elsewhere)

- When a friend spontaneously gives me a same-day invite to get together

- When there is a last-minute change of plans, even as minor as going to a different restaurant than what was planned

- When I don't have access to my special interests and/or comfort items (for me, this includes spending time reading with my favorite blanket, and being able to openly talk about autism, the brain, and behavior, which are my special interests)

- When I need to transition from one activity to another, especially when I am deeply absorbed in an activity

- When I am faced with surprises—good or bad. In other words, probably don't throw me a surprise party.

My challenges in these areas fall directly in line with the autism diagnostic criteria described in the DSM-V. Category B states that to qualify for a diagnosis, the individual must exhibit "restricted, repetitive patterns of behavior, interests, or activities," which can include "insistence on sameness, inflexible adherence to routines, or ritualized patterns of verbal or nonverbal behavior (e.g., extreme distress at small changes, difficulties with transitions, rigid thinking patterns, greeting rituals, need to take same route or eat same food every day)."[1]

The biggest change I've ever faced in my life so far was my transition to motherhood. On a winter's day in 2022, my first baby boy, Lincoln, entered the world. It was a long, 26-hour labor. Matt and I were sleep-deprived and delirious, and complications during delivery led to a traumatic birth experience. Our son had to spend a couple of days in the NICU, which meant I had to be wheeled down every three hours on the dot to nurse him—since I'd chosen to breastfeed and was determined to make it work. This meant even more sleep deprivation on top of everything else.

Finally, on a Friday night, we were discharged and able to take our son home. We bundled him up in the car seat and stepped out of the hospital into the bitter cold February air. Suddenly, there were three of us.

We were back at home and all was dark and quiet. I stepped inside with our new baby and set the car seat down in the middle of our living room floor. Our two cats cautiously approached, sniffing with curiousity. Oh, how I missed the familiarity of our home and our fur babies over those past few days. "It's your new baby brother!" I told them playfully. With tired, swollen eyes, I lifted him out of the car seat, held him, and looked at his sweet, tiny face.

Then I burst into tears.

Reality hit me all at once in that moment. Everything was different. I had a little human to care for and I didn't know what on earth I was doing. No hospital staff or nurses there to direct me. It felt dark, terrifying, and beautiful, all at the same time. After my mini panic attack subsided, Matt and I moved onto our next objective: to try to get some sleep. We swaddled our boy, placed him in the bassinet next to our bed, and finally drifted off into the first full 3-hour stretch that we had experienced in days.

The next day, I woke up disoriented, but I was just happy to see the sun peeking through my window. I was happy to be home, next to my husband. I was happy that our baby was with us and was thriving.

Over the next few weeks, I stepped into a whole new life with a completely different routine. Instead of waking up and going to work, I woke up and nursed. A newborn typically feeds every three hours—at a minimum—and those sessions can last up to 45 minutes, which means there are really only about two hours between each feeding in the beginning.

It was a full-time job I hadn't been remotely prepared for. And since I tend to cling to routine, I quickly began structuring my life around those three-hour intervals—and I was rigid about it.

What I hadn't anticipated was just how much physical contact would be involved in breastfeeding, let alone in caring for a newborn around the clock. Between the soreness of heavy, aching breasts, the constant touching, and the relentless crying, I felt overstimulated almost all the time. And while I know this is something many neurotypical mothers struggle with too, for me—as an undiagnosed autistic woman—it felt extreme. I couldn't understand how other women seemed to get through it without falling apart on a daily basis.

A few days went by. Panic crept in. I felt out of control—this baby had completely overturned my carefully curated daily routines! (Yeah... not sure what I was expecting there.)

I had to start showering in the mornings instead of at night because of the night sweats. I couldn't go out first thing for my caffeine fix: a venti iced coffee with four pumps of vanilla, no classic sweetener, and a splash of cream. I didn't go to work anymore. All of my structure was gone, and I had no idea how to handle it.

And did I mention that hormones are absolutely insane?

The newborn stage still feels very much like a blur in my mind—the bits and pieces that I remember more frightening than happy: sitting on the couch crying and asking Matt if I had made a mistake thinking I could be a mom, attempting to take a shower while listening to my colicky baby scream and cry while his dad tried his best to soothe him, and desperately attempting to hold myself together when family came to visit because I felt so guilty to have been so unhappy after my "bundle of joy" had arrived.

My, how that has all changed. Lincoln is now three years old and is the absolute light of my life. I just had an exceptionally hard time adjusting to all the change. I also was unaware of my personal sensory challenges and made zero accommodations for myself as a result.

Now that I know more about my neurotype, I am working on recognizing sensory overload before I'm, well... completely overloaded. Coincidentally, I made it through postpartum, and I still love motherhood. In fact, I did it all again and gave my firstborn a little brother.

***

While big life changes, like having a new baby, can feel completely derailing to me until a new routine is established, even small,
everyday changes can have a significant impact. Sometimes they
lead to brief moments of emotional dysregulation; other times,
they trigger full-blown meltdowns.

A common theme for me is finding out about a last-minute
change in plans—like choosing a different restaurant after we've
already decided, staying at an event longer than expected, or
being asked to meet up with a friend on the same day. I tend to
freak out initially, but usually manage to regulate after I've had
some time to process the change.

While neurotypicals might feel some discomfort with spontaneity, they're generally able to remain flexible and calm in these
situations. For me, the internal disruption can feel much more
intense and disorienting.

So what do I mean when I say I "freak out" in the face of
change? For me, it feels like a sudden, full-body shift—an intense, physiological surge of energy that comes out of nowhere.
It's a raw irritability, like being trapped in an itchy wool sweater
I can't take off. Pressure builds in my chest and behind my
eyes, and I feel the desperate need to move, to cry, to do something—anything—to let it out.

Imagine a soda can that's been shaken to its limit, ready to
burst. That's what it feels like inside. When I can no longer contain the pressure, it often erupts as a crying spell I can't control.
Once it starts, I have no choice but to ride it out—sometimes for
twenty minutes, other times for over an hour—through waves

of sobbing, yelling, and pacing until the storm finally passes and calm returns.

The good news is that after a meltdown, I usually feel an immense wave of calm. It's almost euphoric—like a long, full-body exhale after holding my breath for too long. It might sound strange, but crying has always been my release valve. Letting the emotions out this way has consistently helped me reset.

The hard part is getting there. Sometimes, the pressure builds for days before it finally spills over, and that buildup is exhausting. I can suppress it for a while, especially in public, but I can't always control when it finally breaks free. And honestly, there are times when I wish it would come sooner, just so I can return to regulation again.

For a long time, I doubted whether I could handle the early days of motherhood a second time and truly thrive. But now I know: I'm far more equipped than I was before. I've learned how to support myself, and my husband has grown alongside me. He understands so much more about autism now and can spot my triggers with greater compassion.

It doesn't mean that I no longer struggle or have meltdowns—I definitely still do. It just means I now have a self awareness that I didn't have before, and it's helped me to take better care of myself.

So if you're neurodivergent and dream of having a family but feel afraid, let this be your reminder: it's possible. And knowing yourself—really knowing yourself—makes all the difference.

***

Helping Yourself

What can you do to make change easier to handle? Here are a few things that I've learned since my diagnosis that may help you:

- **Process before reacting.** Through self-observation, I've noticed over time that my reactions to changes or upcoming plans are always the strongest when I first find out about the change. For example, traveling is hard for me because of the change in environment and routines. It's challenging for me to mentally prepare for a trip, especially one involving groups of people, since I'll have less control on specific day-to-day plans. If I'm told that we're booking a trip with a group, my immediate response is to say no or try to find a reason to avoid participating. However, as time passes, the plan seems just a little less daunting. By the time said dreaded event comes, I am sometimes totally okay with it. Other times, I still feel less than thrilled, but I no longer react with an intense meltdown. Since discovering this, I made the decision to allow those strong emotions to come at the start, but I also hold the thought in my mind that I just need more processing time. I try to let go of my rigid, this-is-set-in-stone-and-there's-no-escape sort of thinking and push myself to a different focal point—maybe

I get back to reading the book I started or watch television. Contrary to how it may seem, I'm not avoiding how I feel, I'm just turning it down a notch by giving myself more time before I perseverate[2] and get stuck in a thought loop. Over the next few days, I can subtly remind myself of what's ahead and process some more, in smaller bits. Each time, the blow of change hits me a little less hard than the time before. Perhaps telling yourself, "This plan is tentative, not set in stone," may help tone it down as well, giving you more time to let the idea marinate when this sort of approach is needed.

- **Practice grounding techniques.** When I react strongly to an upcoming change, I'm moving from a present-moment state to living in the future, whether it be the near future or far-off future. Grounding techniques can be an effective way to help yourself return to reality. The 5-4-3-2-1 involves a quick, 5-step process: naming five things around you that you can see, naming four things around you that you can touch, naming three things that you can hear, naming two things that you can smell, and naming one thing that you can taste.[3] The idea is using your five senses to remind yourself of the present moment. A simpler version, the 3-3-3 method, involves acknowledging three things you can see, three things you can hear, and then moving three parts of your body. There are a variety of strategies you can use, but it's important to identify one simple way to ground yourself that doesn't require too much effort in times of deep stress.

- **Keep comfort items close.** When I know that I'm about to enter an uncomfortable situation that feels too different for me, I bring my own personal sense of familiarity into the new environment. This could be in the form of a comforting item, scent, or activity (for me, this my Kindle, which I bring everywhere I go). Having items or activities that make you feel safe and relaxed can make inevitable change easier to manage.

Helping Your Autistic Loved One

Here are some steps that you may be able to take to make uncertainty easier on your loved one:

- **Make the plan known (and include your loved one in the decision-making process).** If you know your autistic loved one struggles with changes in routine, give them overviews of what is ahead as often as you can. If this is a child or individual who does not have a complex verbal understanding, visual schedules can be useful. If it's an adult with lower support needs, a quick review of the day should suffice. In whatever form you choose, it is also important to include the autistic individual in the planning process when at all possible, allowing for flexibility should the individual choose not to participate in an optional activity when the time comes. This provides them with more cf a sense of control, which is often very comforting for autistics and neurotypicals alike.

- **Offer choices.** While decision-making can, at times, be overwhelming for us, feeling free to express our wants and needs through a genuine sense of openness from others is also a great comfort. Choices allow for increased autonomy (and is especially great for little ones who crave autonomy but cannot have free reign quite yet), but also keeps the range of options smaller, which is great for moments when an infinite number of choices is just too many.

- **Accept boundary-setting in a loving way.** For high-masking autistics like me, it can be challenging to speak up and set boundaries when we are so used to pushing ourselves and trying to fit in with the crowd. Saying no can be extremely hard for me to do and when I finally muster the courage to do it, I often overthink that decision for days. *Was it rude for me to say no? What are they thinking of me? Was my reason good enough?* are the types of thoughts that run through my head. Expressing acceptance and being encouraging when we decide to set personal boundaries can be a big help—it allows us to let gc of those negative thoughts and to have the courage to set boundaries again in the future.

SERENA POGANSKI

Motherhood, Take Two

"Um...Matt? Can you come over here, like now?" A mix of excitement and uncertainty began bubbling up inside me as I gazed upon that white piece of plastic that would somehow reveal how our entire future would change in an instant.

I blinked my eyes again, squeezing them shut tight for a second before trying again to decipher what was in front of me, to make sure my vision was clear. "Does that look like... a second line?" I asked when my husband showed up beside me with the same sort of anticipation written across his face.

"I think so... yes! It definitely is." He said, as his smile appeared—so calm, so easy. And that was the moment we learned that our little family of three was about to grow.

It took me a long time after having our first son to even consider having another. Before we got married, Matt and I always imagined ourselves with two kids in the future—it was an easy, mutual agreement for us. But after having gone through birth trauma and struggling with my mental health postpartum while caring for a baby who seemed to cry for four months straight, we started to question if it was something that we wanted to go through again.

Besides, my once-colicky little baby had turned into the best kid on the face of the earth (okay, maybe I'm a little biased), and I didn't feel that I needed anything more than him. I started telling myself that I was content with just one child and that we wouldn't be having more. All the while, somewhere in the back of my mind, I wondered if that was truly my final decision—if I was really being completely honest with myself.

As I watched Lincoln grow and learn, I began to entertain the thought again. I pictured my little boy as a big brother. I thought about the prospect of him having a best friend for life. I also felt an inkling of sadness each time I thought about the idea that I'd never get to watch a little baby discover a million different firsts ever again.

I was never the type of girl who felt that motherhood was her calling. My transformation—from a girl stuck in her own narrow world to a caregiver responsible for an entire human life—was awkward, uncomfortable, and incredibly disorienting at first. It didn't come naturally to me. But God, I am glad to have experienced it. And when I look at my now 3-year-old and see his kindness, curiosity, and sense of humor, I know then that I must have done something right.

So after a lot of contemplating shortly before Lincoln turned two, I decided I wanted to do this mom thing all over again. Soon after, I became pregnant with Luca.

And when I realized that what was once a mere idea had become a reality, I was met again with questions. Would postpartum be better this time? Would it be worse? Would I really be able to handle the constant demands of having two kids? Would this baby be calm—or would I finally go insane? I thought through every possibility. And yet, underneath it all, there was excitement. Hope. Even a little steady river of optimism.

I wound up opting for a planned c-section after a long period of contemplation filled with hours of research (because, of course, my brain won't allow me to make any serious decision without extensive research). After experiencing birth trauma during my first delivery because of complications, I wanted to take every measure possible to avoid going through anything similar again.

Despite the finality of my decision, I still carried a lot of anxiety leading up to the surgery, as most anyone would. I'd never had any major surgery before, let alone one that involved being cut open while fully awake. The newness of it all drove me to do as much mental preparation as I possibly could.

Beyond educating myself on what would happen before, during, and after the procedure, I listened to hypnosis tracks daily (I had discovered hypnobirthing when preparing for labor with my first baby) so that I could visualize every step involved and create positive associations to a c-section birth.

To the average person, this might just look like me being a type-A, overly prepared person—but for me, the need for predictability and familiarization in the face of new experiences is crucial to maintaining a sense of control and, in turn, calm.

By the time the day came for me to meet my baby, I had imagined it over and over again. I went through each step: checking in, pre-op procedures, and then the daunting walk into the operating room, knowing that within that next hour, I'll have done it. My sweet baby boy would be in my arms and I'd never have to ruminate over getting a c-section again.

He came out with a loud, glorious cry. The minute I saw Luca's face, I could rest. All I could think was, "Thank God. He is well." My decision for delivery felt right. I knew that I still had physical healing left to do, but another sort of healing had already begun.

Immediately after the procedure, I remember being in a state of both awe and overwhelm at all that my body had just gone through. The fact that I had entered the room no more than an hour earlier and now had my baby in my arms was wild to me.

As I was being stitched up, my mind flooded with thoughts—too many to catch or shape into words. I felt frozen, looking back and forth between my husband and my newborn. I tried to open my mouth, to talk about how scary and incredible and amazing the past hour had been, but I was met only with silence. The words were stuck, lodged somewhere too deep to reach.

It was an odd feeling, having so much to say but to suddenly be absent of the ability to translate anything I was feeling into language. I could manage a few short statements, but most everything else felt stuck. When nurses asked me questions as I recovered and the anesthetic began to wear off—"Can you feel this?" they asked, poking at my legs—even answering them felt like an unreasonable amount of effort. I just wanted to sit and process.

The only other time I had experienced anything comparable was during a panic attack or in moments of total overwhelm—when I was burned out, overstimulated, or when my nervous system just couldn't keep up. Following this realization, I discovered that this sort of "verbal shutdown" was yet another common autistic experience.

At one time, I thought of autistic individuals as either speaking or non-speaking. Many of the children that I worked with in the past had no functional spoken language, while others were huge talkers. The idea that there could be an in-between, or that a person's level of verbal communication could shift depending on circumstances, had never occurred to me.

Looking back on my own childhood, I can recall countless moments when words simply wouldn't come. At the time, it was always brushed off as extreme shyness. Maybe it was. Or maybe it was something deeper, something called selective mutism. I still don't know for sure. But now, with a better understanding of my autism, I can look at those moments through a new lens—one that is clearer and more understanding.

In the days and weeks following Luca's arrival, I felt my nervous system shift sharply into a state of hyperarousal. My blood pressure climbed, my heart raced, and my thoughts became a constant swirl—disorganized, restless, and endless. Once again, my world had changed, both externally and within my own body.

But this time, there was something different: awareness. I knew the early days of having a newborn could feel impossible. I knew what challenges might lie ahead. And more importantly, I was aware of my neurodivergence—and ready to give myself the accommodations I hadn't known I needed the first time around.

So this time, I did things like nourish my body with important vitamins and minerals, make time for mindfulness meditations, and wear noise-cancelling headphones when I felt overstimulated. I tuned into my body's signals so that I could catch myself at the first signs of dysregulation rather than waiting until I was in tears dissociating on the couch while holding a crying baby. Needless to say, this newfound awareness transformed my experience as the mother of a newborn.

Granted, the first few months with a new baby come with the expectation of being a hot mess—that's just the reality of broken sleep, leaky boobs, and very little time for self-care. All things considered, I must say I've done rather well.

Simply knowing how my brain works has allowed me to better accept it and work with it, rather than fighting against my own wiring. After many years of believing something was inherently wrong with me—that I was somehow defective for feeling so much anxiety—I've learned instead that my senses are just highly responsive and require protection in chaotic environments. Understanding this has given me a greater sense of control, much like how understanding how a car is built allows you to care for it properly, without forcing parts that don't fit or installing the wrong engine.

Making it through the first few months postpartum without debilitating anxiety or overwhelm felt like a proud accomplishment. I knew what I was doing, I knew what my daily routine would look like, and I felt confident enough to go out and do things with my toddler while wearing the baby in a carrier. Not to mention, Luca was a calm, happy little guy—and this alone had likely saved me from countless meltdowns caused by sensory overload.

Does it make me sad at times that I didn't have the same positive experience with my first baby in the newborn stage as I did with my second? Yes. There are many moments when I am laden with guilt and confusion over the challenge that being a first-time mom had presented me with.

Everyone talks about "baby bliss," the sort of love you had never experienced before, the soaking in of every fleeting moment. I just felt disconnected, alone and afraid at the start of my journey. I adjusted, but it took me longer than expected to feel like myself again.

When I finally did, I found immense joy in this season of life. One of my favorite things to do is watch my children learn. There's a moment of awe I feel when something new is discovered for the first time, when a concept "clicks" into place, or when an idea is brought to life. I am fascinated by my kids' incredible minds—and amazed by how much love I am capable of when it comes to them.

What amazes me even more is how my children can be both the greatest part of my world and, at the same time, my greatest source of overstimulation. Let's be real—kids are loud, sticky, and full of big feelings. And while I had prepared myself for these inevitabilities to some extent, there were other parts of parenting that altered my daily life in ways I hadn't anticipated—ways that made it much harder for me to function anywhere near "normal."

One morning, a few months after we had Luca, I found myself in the kitchen, giving 110% effort to making coffee for myself, breakfast for Lincoln, and tending to the baby, all at once. Moms know that multitasking with kids is overwhelming—there's no argument there. Yet that morning, as I looked around at the remnants of my very first task of the day—an egg-crusted pan on the stove, coffee creamer left open on the counter, and a diaper lying just a few feet shy of the trash can—I couldn't help but wonder why I felt completely drained of cognitive energy by 10 a.m.

My mind had been working so hard to stay on task, yet was constantly tending to interruptions. Doing one thing at a time, yet continually losing track of where I was. Listening to and entertaining my two-year-old, yet struggling to tune out the blare of the stove fan and the sizzle of the frying pan.

Is this how other moms feel? I wondered. Is this normal? It can't be. Other women seem to multitask all day long—but if I spend just an hour scattering my focus too widely, I'm completely burnt out and barely functional for the rest of the day.

I have a habit of going for a coffee run first thing in the morning after the kids have breakfast. I do it because, first of all, it makes me happy. Bought coffee just magically tastes better—one of life's mysteries. And while I probably spend more money on this little routine than I care to admit, I consider it one of the ways I care for my mental health. Caffeine makes me a better mom. I *need* to get out of my house at least once a day, and the predictability of the ritual is soothing. Getting out is like a reset for my brain after a busy morning.

On the days I skip it, I can *handle* the change, sure—but I feel noticeably more dysregulated. This habit actually began when I transitioned to being a stay-at-home mom. For all of my adult life (and even before, during school), I had a routine: wake up, get dressed, do my makeup, and get in the car to go somewhere. That sameness stayed with me for years.

As an autistic person who craves routine, you can imagine how suddenly staying home with a baby completely threw me off. I believe that by keeping the habit of leaving the house each morning, I was holding onto a piece of that old, comforting structure.

It's a little thing, but it might seem odd to others that I would choose to pack up two kids every single day rather than just stay home and relax.

The deeper reason is that luckily, my kids do great in the car and are easily entertained—which gives me the rare opportunity to slip back into a single-focused cognitive state. Being able to focus on one thing at a time is naturally calming for my nervous system and allows my mental energy to recharge after a chaotic morning of constant shifting.

To the outside world, my morning outings might look like just a tired mom treating herself to a coffee. But as you can see, it's so much deeper.

Before I had kids, I was largely unaware of just how much time I spent in a hyperfocused state. It wasn't until that ability—to dive into a task and lose awareness of everything else—was stripped away that I realized how deeply monotropism shaped my mind.

Being a full-time parent means relentless interruptions and endless task-switching. It means starting to prepare a meal, only to stop midway to tend to a crying baby, leaving your meal cold. Then, while soothing the baby, the toddler needs help getting a toy from under the couch. And while you're down there, you notice how badly you need to vacuum—but there's no time, because the baby is getting sleepy and still needs to eat. You finally return to the original task, and within minutes, another interruption pulls you away again. It's never-ending—and especially exhausting for those of us who struggle with executive functioning, where starting, stopping, and switching tasks requires enormous mental energy.

As challenging as it is for me to embrace the wild and bumpy lifestyle my kids have brought into my world, I choose to love it as much as I possibly can. I choose to let it teach me flexibility, to strengthen my resilience, and to shake me up in ways that, at times, leave me feeling like there's nothing left to give. This won't last forever. And in this fleeting time while my children are small, I want to feel it all—to experience every messy, beautiful moment as fully as I can.

I know one day I'll look back with pride and gratitude, remembering all the things I once thought I couldn't do—and

I'll have them to thank for showing me just how much I could grow.

And through it all, I'm reminded: I don't have to become someone else to be the mother they need. God chose me, exactly as I am—neurodivergent, sensitive, deep-feeling—to love them, guide them, and grow right alongside them.

Running Low on Spoons

Today should have been a good day. The weather was nice, I got a solid eight hours of sleep, and my iced coffee was just the right color—not too dark, not too light. I made it through my usual morning routine and while I dragged my feet after forcing myself out of my fluffy blanket nest, I had no suspicions that today would have *not* been a good day.

But after I moved from autopilot mode—get up, brush teeth, wash face, get dressed, do makeup, grab coffee—to needing to use the planning part of my brain to decide what things needed to be done and how to initiate said things, the overwhelm quickly crept in.

Suddenly feeling frozen, I sat down on the couch, pulled out my phone, and distracted myself with social media for a while. In the moment, I didn't realize what I was doing: distracting myself to avoid the stress that came with thinking about my daily tasks—and trading those yucky feelings for a dopamine hit.

Yet all the while, my thoughts were screaming, "Get up and start, you lazy shit!" Harsh, brain. Since when are we a drill sergeant?

I put down my phone, realizing that I was wasting time, as always. I told myself that I needed to just start—just do *something*. I looked around the room. The counters needed to be wiped, I forgot to vacuum yesterday, I had a sticky note on the fridge full of reminders about returning phone calls and emails. But before any of that, I should really clean up the frying pan that's still on the stove from breakfast...

"Mama, I'm done!" My 3-year old said, interrupting my train of thought. He was handing me a plate of breakfast scraps, smiling at me with a ketchup covered mouth.

Being jolted back to the present moment, I took the plate to the sink and started moving. "Why don't you play Legos or color while Mama cleans up? Then we'll play together," I told him .

No more than three seconds into getting the dishes cleaned up, he cries out, "Mama! Play with me!"

"I'll play as soon as I'm done here," I told him. I turned back to the dishes and rushed to quickly get cleaned up.

Okay, got it. Better wipe those counter tops while he's still occupied, I thought. *But wait, if I do that, the floor is going to get covered in crumbs. Maybe I can vacuum quick.* I ran to the closet to grab the vacuum, passing by the laundry room, which contained a basket full of clothes that needed to be put away. They had vanished completely from my memory. Seeing them reminded me that I needed to move the next load to the dryer, too. I did so quickly, wincing at all the different wet, cold textures touching my fingers. Ugh.

"MAMA!!!" I hear again as I'm transferring the last few pieces of clothing.

"I'm coming!" I called back, pressure mounting to just get the damn thing done—before I forgot what I was doing and wound up with a pile of mildew-scented laundry as a result.

I returned to my little boy, knowing he needed some of my time. Instead of having completed the one task that I'd originally set out to do, cleaning up from breakfast, I now had three half-finished things and a completely scrambled brain.

Many of my days go this way. And you might be thinking, "Seriously, just get a planner. Make a routine. Come on."

Executive dysfunction in a neurodivergent brain runs much deeper than just missing an organizational tool that works for everyone else. To review, executive functioning skills include planning, time management, organization, task initiation, flexible thinking, attention and focus, working memory, and self regulation.[1] It's a complex system of skills, but to keep things simple, think of executive functioning as everything you need to effectively get stuff done.

I've seen executive functioning challenges show up in my life since I was school-aged, though I didn't recognize them for what they were at the time. I was always the kid who "had so much potential," but failed to turn in homework or consistently apply myself.

In elementary school, it's normal for parents to take charge of fitting homework into a routine and making sure responsibilities get followed through. That's what made me an A+ student—until that responsibility shifted onto me.

Academics were fairly easy for me, at least in subjects that relied on rote memorization. But anything that required extended focus, sustained attention, and wasn't a strong interest of mine quickly became a lost cause. I excelled in some areas while completely neglecting others.

I went to a private school where classes were so small that everyone knew one another. I was stuck with the same 20ish kids from 1st grade to 8th grade, and then moved to a different private school that was somehow even smaller, to replay the same dynamic for another four years.

In elementary to middle school, Emma Carter was the star student—she always had the best handwriting, took perfect notes, studied hard, and got perfect grades, all while also doing every extracurricular there was. Everything she did seemed to be done perfectly.

Emma and I always seemed to wind up doing the same activities. We were on the volleyball team together, played piano duets at concerts, acted in school plays, and performed in musicals at the same local theater.

I always felt like the sloppy, disorganized, less-put-together version of Emma. She worked hard at school; I only finished my homework if I could squeeze it in during study hall. She answered questions in class while I daydreamed, doodled, and passed notes. She studied and aced every test and I always seemed to be winging it—I couldn't seem to get myself to study for long periods of time because I always got bored.

Our lives seemed so parallel, yet so different. We became friends through it all and looking back, I appreciate the way that she accepted me despite our differences.

When we were young, our moms connected and funny enough, had a bit of a similar dynamic. Emma's mom was structured, organized, and fairly plain. My mom, on the other hand, was a free spirit through and through. She would pull up at the school pickup line in her 1994 Jeep Wrangler, long curly hair wild around her shoulders, wearing beaded jewelry and a smile that looked like summer. Needless to say, she stuck out among the other prim and proper private school moms.

I remember Emma's mom and mine having chats about Emma's study techniques—and even getting a copy of her impressive history notes on a day that I was out sick from school. My mom saw the difference in how she applied herself and worked hard at school, which was when she coined the phrase, "You're just as smart as Emma Carter!"

Back then, she told me this out of frustration, knowing that I *could* have been doing better than I was, had I worked as hard as Emma did. It was irritating, and I'm not sure I truly believed it at the time—nor did I care. Being perfect in school just wasn't that important to me; it always took a back seat to my intense personal interests, like participating in theater. Somehow, though, my mom's phrase stuck. Over the years, it became more of a lighthearted inside joke—and somewhere along the way, I started to believe it a little more.

By the time I reached high school, my executive functioning had started to unravel. Without constant accountability, and with my interests narrowing, I struggled more and more to keep up with responsibilities I didn't truly care about. At this point in time, my sense of self had taken stronger shape. I had more of an idea of who I was and what I cared about—and I was far less willing to pour my energy into things that didn't matter to me.

In high school, I was the quiet, creative type—the kind of kid who drifted off into daydreams during lectures and filled notebooks with poetry. It was the only way I felt I was able to get through sitting in a chair for hours on end , pretending to listen to someone talk about how to find the surface area of a triangular prism.

I remember being repeatedly embarrassed in my English literature class because I never read what I was supposed to for homework. My English teacher had a rule: if you didn't read, you had to leave the classroom and sit in the hallway while the rest of the class discussed the assigned chapters. It got to the point where the teacher would ask me directly at the start of class whether I had done the reading, just to prevent me from picking up answers during the discussion—though cheating never even occurred to me. I didn't see the appeal, or how anyone could feel good about dishonesty.

In my sophomore year of high school, I accidentally signed myself up for an AP (Advanced Placement) anatomy and phys- iology class. I say accidentally because if I'd known it was an AP class, I never would have willingly chosen the heavier workload. In that class, I became the queen of missing assignments. I forgot to do homework so often that, at one point, my teacher mis- placed one of my assignments—but because she was so used to my carelessness, when I insisted I had turned it in, she didn't believe me.

Despite all this, I was able to compensate for my so-called "laziness" by performing exceptionally well in other areas. I remember writing a particularly strong essay on character development in Shakespeare's *Macbeth*. I earned a perfect score and a comment about how well I seemed to understand "the state of the human condition." I hadn't actually read the full material; I read a synopsis and detailed character descriptions and based my essay on what I gleaned from those.

Other times, I saved my grades by doing well on quizzes and tests. As I mentioned earlier, memorization—especially of written information—has always been a strength of mine. While I don't have a full photographic memory, I tend to remember things visually, either as pictures or as text. For example, when I meet someone new and hear their name, I visualize it in text in my mind's eye. When I see that person again later, something about their appearance triggers that text to pop up again. The same thing happens when I try to recall information I've read, which is why I could often glance over notes before a test and still remember what I needed to know.

Yet in classes where success depended less on memorization and more on learning new and shifting concepts, like algebra or chemistry, I couldn't keep up. I struggled to pay attention day after day, promised myself I'd focus better tomorrow, and still repeatedly failed to do so. I resorted to "teaching myself" by reading the textbook and watching endless YouTube tutorials. I learned better this way because I could move at my own pace, rereading the same algebraic step as many times as I needed until it finally clicked. Still, in these subjects, I consistently struggled and had to put in far more effort. Here, my executive dysfunction really showed—because unlike with some subjects, I couldn't just "wing it" when it came to complex formulas.

You might be thinking I should be good at math since I'm autistic. Well, here I am to debunk another classic stereotype: not all of us got the "good with numbers" flavor of autism. While I absolutely love data, graphs, and statistics (because I *love* information), I'm not necessarily great at calculating them myself. I call myself a numbers admirer, not a numbers genius.

All of this is to say that when it came to school, there were areas where I performed exceptionally—and others where I struggled significantly. Because I had shown that I was capable of impressive work, my shortcomings were usually framed as laziness or a lack of effort.

I'll admit that I could have tried harder. A big part of the problem was simply that I didn't care enough. Yet the funny thing is, I *wanted* to care. I remember clearly wishing I could push through subjects that bored me, but I couldn't understand how others managed to stay so focused and interested across so many different areas at once.

I've always had a few, very intense interests at a time. When it comes to anything outside those fixed interests, I have to push myself hard to stay motivated—and even when I want to care, I often can't make myself. I live in extremes, pulled always toward all or nothing. When motivation is there, I soar. When it's not, I struggle. To put it simply: my performance mirrors my passion.

Explaining that this is my tendency is, of course, not an excuse for underachievement. In fact, I've never seen it that way—and because of my repeated failed attempts to get it together in school, I labeled myself as lazy. What I didn't know until just a few years ago was that my neurotype has an impact on both motivation and executive functioning.

To break it down, autistic individuals often need extra support with executive functioning skills like planning, organization, time management, task initiation, and flexible thinking. This is largely due to differences in the prefrontal cortex—the part of the brain responsible for these functions.

Most autistic people also have a more monotropic thinking style, meaning they focus intensely on a few subjects at a time. Because of this, traditional schooling, which requires students to divide their attention across many subjects simultaneously, can be inherently more challenging.

A closely related neurotype that often occurs alongside autism is ADHD (Attention-Deficit/Hyperactivity Disorder). While this isn't a book about ADHD, it's worth mentioning, since estimates suggest that somewhere between 50% to 80% of autistic individuals also meet the criteria for ADHD.[2]

Sustaining motivation can be especially difficult for ADHDers, which can be explained in part by the dopamine theory of ADHD.[3] According to some research, ADHD is associated with lower levels of dopamine—the "feel-good" neurotransmitter that surges when we do things that bring us pleasure. Dopamine is directly linked to motivation: when we accomplish a task and feel rewarded, dopamine reinforces that behavior.

For individuals with ADHD, however, motivation tends to depend more on pleasure, novelty, challenge, or urgency, creating what some call an "interest-based" nervous system. In contrast, neurotypicals tend to operate with an "importance-based" system, allowing them to prioritize what needs to be done, even when those tasks carry no strong emotional interest.

As you can imagine, all of these factors can easily create the perfect executive dysfunction storm. Being diagnosed with autism and/or ADHD doesn't mean you're doomed to a lifetime of struggling with planning, organization, and staying on top of important tasks—but it does certainly create some resistance.

In high school, I didn't understand why it seemed harder for me to stay motivated and interested compared to my peers. I resorted to believing that I was simply lazy and that it was all my fault. Eventually, I gave up trying to do better and instead, fully embraced the parts of school that I actually enjoyed: theater, art, writing, daydreaming.

I took nothing else seriously, but I still had ideas of what I wanted to do with my life, and I kept telling myself, *I can't wait until I can go to college and study things I actually care about!* Apparently, I wasn't wrong—finding a focused area of study made a world of difference for me. Once I discovered my passion for psychology, I was all in. I ended up graduating with a 4.0 GPA.

Today, executive dysfunction affects me in different ways. For the past three years, I've been a stay-at-home mom. It wasn't part of my original plan by any means, but I adore my children, and it made sense for many reasons to take this extra time while they are young.

Household duties, however, have never felt exciting to me. Some people enjoy cleaning and homemaking. Some people dream of that sort of life. While I absolutely need a tidy home in order to feel calm and focused, I *hate* chores. I don't enjoy doing them, and I don't feel much of a sense of accomplishment when they're done—just relief.

Not falling too far behind is crucial for my mental health; clutter is extremely overstimulating to me, and a backlog of tasks makes even beginning feel unreasonably overwhelming.

But having young children means that falling behind at times is practically inevitable. It also means *lots* of interruptions, which results in constant starting and stopping of tasks, shifts in routine, and unexpected disasters (think a roll of toilet paper in 1,000 tiny pieces all over the floor after just five minutes of leaving a toddler unattended). It's the opposite of consistent and organized—the very conditions my autistic brain needs in order to thrive.

Some days, it feels like my energy is slipping away faster than I can catch it. Spoon Theory, a metaphor often used in chronic illness and neurodivergent spaces, helps it make more sense.[4] The idea is that each day, you wake up with a limited number of "spoons," or units of energy. Every task—doing the dishes, folding laundry, making a phone call—costs a spoon (sometimes more than one). And when you're out of spoons, you're out. There's no pushing through. You simply have nothing left to give. For me, each day feels like a delicate balancing act, as I try to stretch a limited supply of energy across a life that demands so much.

For the past three years, I've been trying to figure out how everyone seems to manage this stay-at-home mom life without losing their minds.

Learning about my brain was the only thing that finally made it all make sense. I've decoded my vicious cycle of buying new planners or trying out new life hacks every few months, totally convinced that *this time* I'm about to change my life—only to crash and burn under a mountain of laundry soon after, then repeat it all again, hoping for a different outcome.

I may never perfect my life. I may always require two to three business days to move my laundry from the washer to the dryer to the closet. I may never wake up one morning and decide that I've finally grown into my true domestic nature and that cleaning and tidying are my new favorite zen activities. I may always prioritize my special interests over whatever the most responsible thing to get done is.

Still, with each passing year, I seem to get just a bit closer to making my lifestyle work in harmony with my brain. In a way, this dynamic parallels the rest of my life: struggling significantly in some areas while performing above and beyond in others.

Even now, with all the insight I've gained, I still have moments where I feel like I'm falling short—like I'm not measuring up to some invisible standard. But it's in those moments that I try to remind myself of how far I've come. Sure, I've missed a lot of assignments. I've forgotten about the laundry way too many times. I've lost my cool because of my complete inability to multitask.

But really? None of that has stopped the world from turning—or stopped me from being successful in the ways that actually matter to me.

Now, my mom sometimes says to me, "I told you that you were just as smart as Emma Carter!"

It usually happens when I share an accomplishment, overcome a challenge, and most importantly, when I'm feeling less than competent. I think that's when I need to hear it most.

***

Helping Yourself

Here are some practical ways you can support your own executive functioning:

- **Break down tasks into micro-steps.** Large tasks can feel daunting and may cause us to freeze or avoid getting started. Instead of putting a broad goal, like cleaning the kitchen, on the to-do list, break it down into smaller steps. For example: 1) wipe counters, 2) wipe appliances, 3) do dishes, 4) mop floors. Each individual step can be broken down further, as many times as is needed!

- **Use external reminders.** Lists, timers, phone reminders, and sticky notes are absolutely crucial for me when it comes to getting stuff done! Use them and use them often. I especially find *pomodoro timers* to be useful.

- **Create flexible schedules.** Autistic brains thrive when routines are put in place, but ADHD brains tend to resist them, creating a hard-to-win battle for people with dual diagnoses. A flexible schedule is a perfect in-between. Consider creating "task blocks" within your day, where you'll have the freedom to choose what you want to tackle first.

- **Try body doubling.** This refers to simply having another person work alongside you (doing their own thing), which can help boost focus and productivity.

- **Respect your spoons.** Remember that every task you take on uses up some amount of energy. Budget accordingly, honor your personal limits, and prioritize rest—which can help restore lost spoons.

Helping Your Autistic (or Neurodivergent) Loved One

- **Provide the right tools.** Rather than trying to micromanage, introduce your loved one to a variety of tools and strategies that might support their executive functioning—planners, apps, timers, visual schedules, sticky notes—and encourage them to experiment and see what feels right for them.

- **Normalize sensory breaks and rest.** Remember that taking regular breaks and resting is actually very important for managing energy and preventing burnout. You can support your loved one by respecting their need for still, quiet moments, or even helping build downtime into their daily routine.

- **Understand that task-switching is draining.** Shifting focus between tasks can be mentally exhausting for a neurodivergent brain. Whenever possible, allow your loved one to fully finish one task before mentioning the next. Keeping the focus on one step at a time can make a big difference in reducing overwhelm.

- **Use positive reinforcement.** Instead of focusing on what still needs to get done, highlight successes—even the small ones. Pointing out moments when helpful tools were used or when tasks were completed, no matter how minor they seem, can help build momentum and encourage continued progress.

The People Pleasing Paradox

Beneath my easy smile and polite nods, another truth was always stirring: the deep, relentless need to forge my own path.

For many years, I lived as a chronic people pleaser. I stayed quiet when I wanted to speak, put other people's preferences above my own, and endured discomfort for the sake of not inconveniencing anyone else.

While I'm learning to leave the people pleasing behind, one thing that has stayed with me is my immense craving for control in all aspects of my life. I like to have full control when it comes to anything I consider to be my responsibility, to the point where I often refuse to ask for help.

I can't stand plans being sprung upon me that aren't my own. I don't like feeling bound to anyone else's agenda—I like to know that I have the freedom to choose what to do with my time and when to do it. As you can see, it's a bit of a paradox. How can someone so deeply crave freedom but also spend so long shaping themselves to fit everyone else's needs?

There is a difference between people pleasing and having a healthy amount of consideration of what others want. There is also a difference between having a pathological need for control and setting healthy boundaries. Somehow I've lost my own sense of safety by constantly darting between the two extremes.

I've done this for years without any sort of awareness of my behavior—until I learned about the terminology used to describe these experiences, and that neurodivergent individuals are often very familiar with this people pleasing paradox.

PDA traditionally stands for pathological demand avoidance, a profile of autism characterized by a persistent, intense need for control.[1] In more recent years, it's been reframed as persistent drive for autonomy—wording that feels both more accurate and more respectful to many autistics.[2]

In my own work, I've seen many children who seemed to fit this profile clearly. How does PDA show up in a young child? I typically look for behaviors like insisting on controlling play scenarios and becoming very upset when others try to change the sequence; repeatedly refusing to do anything presented as a demand, even activities they typically enjoy; or disliking praise and external rewards.

Much too often, PDA profile children are mistaken as defiant or manipulative. Parents are wrongly blamed for their supposed lack of discipline. But when you understand autism at its core, the picture becomes much clearer.[3]

To autistics, the world can feel too loud, too disorganized, too intense. Now imagine how a child—still new to the world, still learning how to feel, to share, to be the tiniest bit independent—experiences this wild life as a being who needs the comfort of control and routine to feel safe.

As a little girl, I was resistant to change, newness, and out-of-the-blue adventures. My mother, who is still far more spontaneous than I am to this day, spent much of my childhood filling our days with fun. She tells me she would wake me up and excitedly ask, "Serena, do you want to go to the zoo today?!" or "It's a sunny day! Want to go to the pool?" And without fail, I always said no.

She never really understood it, because after much coaxing and encouragement, I would eventually give in, agree to go, and usually end up having a good time. "You just needed a little push to realize you liked things," she'll tell me. I've heard these stories for years, all circling the same theme: I was cautious, fearful of new things, and resistant to the unfamiliar.

This is how my need for sameness first showed it-self—through quiet, cautious inhibition. Because I was a girl, I was simply labeled "timid." But if I had been a boy, would that resistance have looked different? Would it have shown up as yelling, fighting, or running away? Possibly.

As I entered my teenage years, the need for autonomy start-ed to burn hot. Around age thirteen, I began doing a little more on my own—going to the mall with friends, getting dropped off at the movies—and I fear I liked my small taste of freedom a little too much.

I hated asking permission for everything, and I hated being told no even more. Every denied request felt like a personal attack on my freedom, and as a result, resentment toward my parents grew.

I just didn't listen when it came to responsibilities, and being pressed with reminders only made me dig my heels in deeper. I remember mentally planning to start chores at a specific time—only to have my motivation evaporate the instant my mom brought them up first. Suddenly, no way was I doing it now.

Consequences like losing my phone or getting grounded didn't work either; they just turned everything into a bigger, more dramatic battle. Add teenage hormones and emotional dysregulation to the mix, and... well. I was a walking disaster zone. (Sorry, Mom. Truly.)

My tendency to keep the world feeling as predictable as possible has followed me into adulthood. The difference now, as a 31-year-old, is that I finally have more control over what my days look like. I make my own schedule, curate my environment exactly how I want it, and choose what activities I do—and when. Obviously, these are all abilities that are limited to us in our childhood.

My need for control shows up in ways that create real challenges for me, especially when it comes to interpreting interactions with others. Being aware of my own rigidity can make it harder to trust my own perspective—it's like I'm constantly flipping between seeing a situation through someone else's eyes and through my own, never quite sure which version is more reasonable.

I know that people are a complicated mix of learned behavior, cultural influences, personal motives, and care for others. We all view things through our own distinct lenses. I also know that when something feels like a threat to my independence, whether it's real or perceived, I can respond irrationally. And if I can't trust others or myself, how do I know when a boundary actually needs to be set?

Time and time again, I am faced with the confusion of decoding both social norms and my own behavior in a desperate attempt to be fair and understanding. I might get caught in a spiral like this:

"I'll be stopping by in a few hours!"

Um... excuse me?! That wasn't on my schedule. You can't just drop that on me. This is not okay. Why would you push something on me like this? It's my life.

Wait... am I overreacting? No. Other people would feel the same, right? I mean, plenty of people would be upset if someone just invited themselves over.

But is it different because it's family? Why does that matter?

God, I hate that I don't say anything. I've never been good at setting boundaries—how would anyone even know what mine are?

I'm just being ridiculous. I suck. I suck. I suck.

This is just an example of what goes through my head when I'm trying to figure out how to respond to something that feels, to me, like it's impeding upon my sense of control. It involves the constant push-pull of wanting to take back control while also desperately wanting to make sure that other people remain happy with me.

This brings me to the other side of the coin—a truth I've tried to ignore for a long time: feeling rejected by others hurts me far more deeply than I care to admit.

And yes, I know rejection is painful for most people. But I, along with many other neurodivergent individuals, feel it at a completely different level. Even the slightest ounce of detected criticism or rejection—a passing remark or change in tone—can burn like salt inside an open wound.

I like to imagine that I am unaffected by people. I tend to live in a world of my own and generally, I like it that way. I like to choose exactly how to spend my time. I like to get sucked into interesting topics until reality seemingly fades away. I have found peace in a simple life with my partner and my little family.

But the truth is, my relationship with people is more complicated than it seems.

Aside from those I hold very close, I don't often let others in. I show up quietly, agreeable and easygoing. I smile and nod. I let other people talk and talk about themselves until they turn blue in the face. I then get deemed a "great listener"—sometimes people think they like me because I will sit and listen, rarely challenging their thoughts or ideas.

What I think they actually like is having the stage. And in a world where it can be hard to really be heard, that's fair.

Slowly, I make small attempts to share more of myself—to let my true self peek through the surface. But I do it carefully and deliberately. I've learned to curate my language and mannerisms to match the other person, to make them feel safe and at ease. Based on past interactions, I observe what's welcomed and what's not, adjusting accordingly—all in an effort to stay connected without causing discomfort. I do all of this until I get sick of it, of trying so hard to please.

Eventually, there's always a breaking point—an opinion I hold too strongly, a moment when I just can't contain myself behind the mask anymore, or a boundary that gets crossed and pushes me to drop the people-pleasing act altogether.

I start showing up as I truly am. And suddenly, the quiet, agreeable persona I've created changes. People are surprised to find that I am quite the opposite of the character I've tried to keep intact.

I'm particular. I need structure and control in order to function well. I have unshakable opinions and firm beliefs. I'm kind but honest—and sometimes people are offended by honesty. I'm logical but deeply passionate—and often being passionate is seen as obsessive. I want to connect with people, but sometimes the way I do it is seen as "oversharing." I've spent so long trying to present myself in the most palatable way possible, and the constant effort of masking is utterly exhausting.

I've found that when I finally do unmask around other people, it tends to happen suddenly and unexpectedly—usually when I'm overwhelmed or feel like I'm losing control.

For example, after several unexpected drop-ins from a friend, I might suddenly blurt out, "I really can't handle the unplanned visits—can you please ask me to make plans ahead of time from now on?"

The friend, who thought I was the easygoing, go-with-the-flow type I'd been trying to appear as, would likely be completely thrown off. "What's gotten into her? Why so rigid all of a sudden?" she might think.

Then comes the discomfort—not the expected discomfort that comes with a moment of boldness and passes just as quickly, but the debilitating, hollow feeling that comes with the anticipation of brutal, unkind rejection.

Any time I allow myself to open the door to conflict, I feel like a snake shedding its skin. Vulnerability is incredibly hard for me because I am constantly perceiving rejection in some sort of way. Every word that I speak lingers, etched in the corners of my mind to be scrutinized later by the version of myself that is insecure, unequipped, questioning. Every response from others is also recalled and played back over and over like scenes from a movie—an endless loop of second-guessing.

Sometimes I can't help but formulate imagined assumptions that I expect others to hold against me based on my own over-analysis of our interactions. Where does this all come from?

Perhaps from a lifetime of practice dissecting the behavior of those around me—carefully watching other people's social volleys in attempts to one day uncover the secret to seamless conversation.

Maybe I've decoded excessively. Or maybe I really do struggle to interpret social cues the way many autistic people are said to. If I can't easily grasp what someone is thinking, maybe my brain fills in the blanks with its own story.

Maybe it stems from a lifetime of feeling misunderstood—so much so that I've come to assume I'm always being misunderstood, even when I'm not. Maybe I fixate on people's inner worlds because understanding humans is one of my deepest special interests, and I mistakenly assume that everyone else cares just as much about the inner workings of the mind as I do.

Whatever the reason, it seems that caring so much has done more harm than good. Caring about what people think has done nothing but restrict me to a life at the mercy of others' approval. And even by doing that, I have lost control over my own ability to just be me.

So it's no wonder I seek control in other ways—through routine, through ownership of my responsibilities and work, through often choosing solitude, where I won't be perceived, judged, or questioned. When you consider both the social dynamics I've described and the neurological differences many autistic people share, the desire to live life on our own terms feels not just understandable—but completely reasonable.

The intensity with which we chase control often depends on how safe we feel in our own skin—which also influences how much we're able to live unmasked. The more we feel the need to pretend, the more we need to compensate for that lack of safety by creating some of our own.

How does my persistent drive for autonomy show up in my life? In exactly that way: overcompensation. Because I'm autistic, I need to know all the details before entering a new scene—just to mentally process each transition. If there's a social gathering, I want to know exactly when it starts, who's coming, and what the order of events will be. I like to know what the environment will feel like so I can be prepared.

To a neurotypical person, that might seem excessive or unnecessary. Without the understanding that I'm autistic, this kind of behavior often gets labeled—stiff, rigid, Type A—and over time, we start to internalize those labels. I spent most of my life before my diagnosis watching others appear to effortlessly "go with the flow," and tried to force myself to do the same. It didn't work for me, and I saw that as failure. Every time my rigidity cropped up, I met it with shame.

Then I started to mask. I did everything I could to blend in because I believed that being easygoing was the "right" way to be. Over time, I had myself trained to appear one way on the outside while experiencing a whole different internal reality, and a mountain of discomfort beginning to stew inside of me.

I remember being with boyfriends, trying so hard to be "fun." I remember being told that I needed to let go, be spontaneous, and experience more adventure. I heard this plea so many times that I started to believe it—that being an off-grid thrill seeker would somehow make my life better.

I remember being at sleepover parties as a little girl, trying to have fun and be cool, but just wanting to go home to my own bed.

I backed out of things like middle school retreats, traveling abroad with my Spanish class, and going on a senior trip in high school, just because I had no interest and found it all to be too much change. Everyone asked me why, appearing half concerned and half offended. I didn't exactly have an answer, but I felt that whatever the reason, it was wrong.

I guess I'm just weird. It was a label I accepted before I knew I was autistic—one I still claim today, though now with pride!

Masking my discomfort in the face of change didn't make the discomfort disappear. Instead, it pushed me to overcompensate by clinging even harder to control—taking extreme measures to ensure that I've taken back control where it was missing for me.

Instead of just asking for more details about upcoming events, I began refusing to go altogether—or even putting together my own events just so that I could be in charge of how everything looked and felt.

Instead of being honest about my needs with others, I decided I would just do everything myself. To this day, receiving help can feel like a threat to my competence. (Yes, I know—it's a weakness I'm aware of, and I'm working on it.)

For a long time, two sides of me have fought one another: the desire to be in control of my life and the desire to be likeable. I thought that the two simply could not coexist—that being likeable depended on how much of my comfort I could sacrifice in order to avoid sticking out or appearing to be demanding.

Intellectually, I now understand that this is a false and damaging belief, but letting go of that pattern in practice has been incredibly hard.

I'm learning that with the right people, I can be particular and still be loved. But I'd be lying if I said I wasn't happiest in my own company. Being alone is easy—I don't have to worry about saying the wrong thing or losing control over my day. I can focus fully on whatever inspires me in the moment—usually a topic that I'm highly invested in.

Being alone recharges me, fills my cup, and allows me the capacity to then return to those whom I love and give them the best version of me.

Those rare people who truly see me—the ones who already understand what I need to feel grounded—make it possible for me to simply exist, unmasked. Their presence has made my world softer, safer, and more whole.

I may forever feel like I'm walking on a tightrope, trying to balance between control and connection, but I'm learning that I don't have to choose one or the other. I can be both fully loved and fully free—and perhaps that is the purest love there is.

Out of Sight, Not Out of Heart

You know the saying, "Birds of a feather flock together"? I've come to believe it's true—especially when it comes to people like me. Somehow, those of us with brains that work a little differently always seem to find one another. I didn't realize it at the time, but most of the close friends I had growing up likely weren't neurotypical either. Looking back now, it's easy to see how different the people I naturally gravitated toward really were. It's a funny, but somehow comforting, realization.

The dynamics of friendship have never come naturally to me. The best way I can describe it is that most people seem to operate like automatic cars when it comes to social relationships—while I'm stuck with manual transmission. I have to consciously think through the steps of building a relationship: gauging what's appropriate to talk about, trying to figure out what stage we're at in the relationship, and often pre-planning conversations ahead of time. As you can imagine, it takes a lot more effort than it probably should.

Except for those rare moments when I meet someone I instantly click with. It doesn't happen often, but when it does, it feels like a notable event. I'll come home and tell my husband, "Wow, I talked to someone today and didn't feel weird at all! The conversation actually flowed, and I even enjoyed myself!" These interactions feel almost magical.

I figured out by the time I was 29 and got my diagnosis that this sort of thing probably isn't normal. That's when I started asking myself, "What do all these people that I've instantly clicked with have in common?"

Hmm... didn't that girl in high school fixate on the same things I did? And she always rocked back and forth when she was standing—that was definitely a stim.

Oh, and I clicked with so-and-so because she was totally fine doing the exact same thing every time we hung out. Routine felt good to both of us.

My autism radar was officially activated.

Of course, I say all this lightly. I'm not trained in diagnosing other people and can't assume that all my good friends were neurodivergent. But looking back, there's a high likelihood that many of them were, or at least shared some similar traits.

One of my current good friends falls into this category. When I first met Jade, I was blown away by how easy it was to talk with her. I had taken my son to our local Barnes & Noble—one of his favorite places—and as we headed to the children's section, he locked eyes with an adorable, chubby blonde toddler girl. They exchanged smiles, and soon her mom, who would become one of my closest friends, walked over.

My son was instantly drawn to both Jade and her daughter, trailing behind them and watching with curiosity. Eventually, he approached, and Jade and I began chatting—*Are you from this area? Are you a stay-at-home mom too? How old is your kid?*—the typical small talk that I had gotten used to having since becoming a mom.

But Jade had a different vibe about her. During most of my social exchanges with new people, I often feel like I'm putting on a performance. I don't mean that to say I'm ungenuine or don't enjoy talking to people—I just don't always feel safe enough to be my authentic self. After masking for so long, I'm not entirely sure how people would respond to the person underneath it all.

Yet when I talked to Jade, I felt comfortable. I sensed there was a real chance that she might accept my true self, even if I couldn't explain why. It was just a feeling.

At the end of our time interacting, we exchanged numbers and talked about having another playdate for the kids. And that was that.

We've been getting together most weeks since. By our second time meeting up, we got into topics including religion, mental health, self-improvement, and other niche interests. I went home feeling invigorated—happy that we skipped over the dreaded small talk pretty quickly. I also had a sneaking suspicion that she, too, might have been neurodivergent.

By our third hangout, I shared with her that I'd recently received an autism diagnosis. I did it because I figured, what do I have to lose? I had entered the new year vowing to start working on unmasking. I'd been praying and hoping for an authentic friendship. I decided it was time to experiment with not caring what others might think of me, for once. If being myself scared someone off, what did it matter? Her response: "I think I might be autistic, too!" Ah, sweet relief. This lady didn't think I was crazy.

Being more open about my challenges has been healing, and experiencing acceptance as my unmasked self is giving me more confidence to keep working at allowing that part of me to come out from the shadows.

My friend Jade may share some of my own traits, which makes the process easier, but neurotypes aside, she has been an incredibly caring friend—someone who looks beyond the surface and seeks to know others in a deep, intentional way. Those are the kinds of people that I want in my life. So now, I'm choosing not to worry about who wanders away for trivial reasons.

So in what ways can navigating friendships be difficult for someone like me? After contemplating this, I discovered that the answer is multilayered and comes down to four core factors: social expectations, communication differences, ability to connect, and executive functioning.

Social Expectations

I've only just recently realized that neurotypical expectations are different from mine where friendship is concerned. For many people, friendship is a sort of commitment that involves "checking in" and seeing one another at least semi frequently. In other words, it's something that needs to be maintained—something that can disintegrate over time.

Yet in my mind, if you were ever once my friend, I still would consider you a friend many years later, even if we hadn't talked. To this day, I think fondly of friends that I've had in high school or from previous jobs, and I don't feel that I've abandoned my care for them, despite failing to check in.

I'm caught off guard when others feel differently. There has been a time or two that I reached out to an old friend after many years of silence, asking how they have been. On some occasions, the responses were positive. Other times, I sensed that the other person felt I had left them in the dust and perhaps that I had ulterior motives for contacting them, seemingly out of nowhere.

So what makes keeping in touch so difficult? Usually, what happens is I simply forget. I may have read the last text while I was busy or deeply absorbed in something else and told myself that I would respond later. Then I never responded because the message got lost in a mess of other messages I hadn't responded to. Then I remembered that we were in the middle of a conversation approximately two weeks later and decided it would be too late to backtrack at that point. So what do I do? Never talk to that person again, I suppose. An airtight system, really.

Another reason I may fail to properly maintain friendships is because the concept of "missing" others feels...almost rare for me. Anecdotal information I've gathered from the neurodivergent community suggests this may be a common experience due to impaired object permanence—the awareness that something (or someone) still exists even when it's not right in front of you.

Autistics and ADHDers alike often experience this "out of sight, out of mind" phenomenon. I recognize it in myself with both objects and people—if I put away my crocheting materials, even after a solid week of hyperfixating on them, I suddenly forget they exist and lose interest.

I need visual reminders for everyday tasks. I also need to see someone regularly to remember how much I enjoy their company. Just admitting this brings feelings of shame. It's hard not to equate the absence of longing with the absence of love.

"You mean you don't miss family and friends? Don't you care?"

Please don't mistake this for a lack of affection. I often think of loved ones fondly and genuinely enjoy our time to-gether—but having a very one-track mind means I have to pause from a state of hyperfocus to let other thoughts in. When I'm deeply immersed in whatever I'm doing, it's easy to lose track of time and distance, and I don't always find space to wonder when I'll connect with people again. But when I do pause and reflect, my feelings are clear—because my love runs deep.

So while a lack of contact does not deteriorate the relation-ship for me, it may do so for that other person. I have grieved for the friendships that could have been—the ones that never took root, never thrived because of the actions I didn't take. And if you're reading this and happen to be one of those people on the other side, I truly am sorry if I made you feel underappreciated. I see it now, and I'm working on it.

Connection & Communication

One of the core traits associated with autism is differences in communication.[1] And since friendship is largely built upon back-and-forth social exchanges in order to connect, this can create some challenges.

So what sorts of communication differences might an autistic person have? The range, like the spectrum as a whole, is large. A high-masking person like me might just appear awkward or shy.

Others, who are more extroverted, may spew out thoughts that could be deemed "socially inappropriate" or brain dump about their special interest in polar bears for much longer than the other party is interested, missing cues that say, "I'm bored." To get into more detail, I have categorized the ways that I, and other autistics, might encounter communication challenges regularly:

Narrow Interests

By nature, I tend to narrow my array of personal interests to just a few things at a time, meaning I focus my attention very heavily on the few things that matter deeply to me, while paying very little attention to other things. My current special interests revolve around autism, the brain, and psychology—topics I can talk about endlessly. Yet, I am very socially aware in the sense that I understand most other people don't always want to hear me ramble about them, so I'm often quiet in groups.

While neurotypicals more naturally bounce between light-hearted topics like weather, movies, current events, and pop culture, I simply don't enjoy these sorts of conversations and feel utterly lost when it comes to taking part in them; I don't really know how to contribute.

Instead, I might zone out, retreating into my own little mental world, quietly spinning through the things I'm passionate about. On the outside, I can sometimes appear withdrawn. Other times, I may seem present but unopinionated—exactly why people like to tell me I'm such a great listener.

Timing and Turn-Taking

Another challenge I face in social groups is knowing when it's my turn to talk—or just finding a second to chime in. This is a challenge commonly brought up within the autistic community and for the longest time, I couldn't pick apart why it can be so hard for us. You wait for a short pause, then speak, right?

I attribute this challenge to both analytical thinking and delayed processing.[2] The autistic part of me prefers to think deeply before speaking (sometimes a little too much) and to prepare for how others might respond. I do this because I'm soothed by predictability and dislike being put on the spot. But that takes time—and by the time I'm ready to speak, the conversation has often already moved on. Add in the delayed processing from trying to tune out background noise or distracting visuals, and it's easy to fall behind.

As a result, I either interrupt people unintentionally or stay quiet altogether. To others, I might seem disengaged or uninterested.

Compared to group conversations, I do much better in one-on-one settings, where it's easier to tell when it's my turn to speak, there's less to keep track of, and I have more freedom to pause and think.

Social Decoding

Before I say what I'm about to say, I know it makes me sound a little bit like a "I'm not like other girls" type of girl, but it's the truth: I've always found it much easier to get along with men than with women. Why? Men are generally more direct and straightforward when it comes to communicating—there is a lot less reading between the lines involved. Women don't always mean exactly what they say. Their language is often multilayered: what's said, what's implied, and what's expressed don't always align.

People like to believe that autistics just flat-out miss social cues, which *may* explain why straightforwardness is usually appreciated. But in my experience, it's not that I miss cues; it's that I pick up on too many of them. I can be overly aware, almost hyper-attuned to subtleties that even neurotypicals might overlook—and noticing things like expressions or body language that seem to contradict what is being said makes interpretation very confusing.

A classic example is the immediate "sense" I sometimes get about a person upon first meeting them. I can tell when something feels off or disingenuous, even if I can't explain exactly why—and I'm usually right. Others may not notice it at all and assume I'm being judgmental... until something obvious happens that reveals the person's true intentions.

I might hear something like, "Gosh, I guess you were right about them, Serena."

Strong pattern recognition may be part of the reason. Research suggests that brain regions responsible for pattern detection are more active in autistic individuals compared to the general population.[3] This might help explain why so many autistics excel in areas like math, science, music, or problem-solving.

But pattern recognition isn't limited to academic strengths—it shows up in human behavior, too. Even when I'm not consciously aware of it, small changes in someone's tone, facial expression, or posture often register in my brain and stick there. Then later, in a completely different context, those cues resurface and I just know something is off.

Another example: I get *so* thrown off by the "customer service voice"—you know, the obligatory, overly enthusiastic tone you're supposed to use when working with customers? I used to do it when I worked in retail (and honestly, I was pretty good at it). But when I am on the other side as the customer, it just leaves me feeling confused and uncomfortable. It's like my senses say, "Something about this is inauthentic—which doesn't feel safe."

When I pull up to Starbucks and the bubbly barista greets me with an unnaturally cheerful, "How are you today?!" I simply follow the social script.

"Great, thank you! How are you?" Easy and predictable.

But once in a while, they go off the usual script and start asking about my plans for the day, or what's new—and that's when I freeze. Like I said, I'm bad at improv. And I usually need a second to process the sudden shift from a meaningless, routine sort of interaction to an actual conversation, so sometimes my responses can come out a bit awkward.

On the other hand, there are moments when I'm greeted by someone at a store or café with a neutral, "Hey, how's it going?" and an unreadable face—and strangely, I find that kind of honesty soothing. It feels easier to understand someone when their expression isn't layered with social expectations.

While it's certainly not always the case, I've found that women's outward expressions more often differ from what they're really feeling, whereas men tend to be a bit more transparent. Maybe that's part of why many of my closest friendships, especially growing up, were with boys. They just felt easier to read.

Executive Functioning and Matching Dynamics

A final challenge when it comes to friendship is how executive dysfunction can affect both motivation and planning—making it harder to maintain regular contact or follow through with social plans. Organizing a simple get-together might seem easy to most, but to me, it can feel like *a lot*.

First of all, let's review what all executive functioning entails to get a better sense of how these areas can be related. Executive functioning skills include things like planning, time management, organization, task initiation, flexible thinking, attention and focus, working memory, and self- regulation.[4] Struggles in these areas are common for individuals with autism and/or ADHD, though how they show up varies from person to person. Personally, while I face challenges across several of these domains, a few of them tend to impact me more frequently than others.

One particular trait that has presented me with the most challenge throughout my life is my rigid style of thinking. I am a planner, I thrive off of routine, and I don't like it when things change suddenly. This becomes tricky when making plans with people who thrive on last-minute decisions and spontaneity. I want an agenda; they want to see where the day takes them. I want a specific time; they don't need one. I prefer short outings; they 're picturing an all-day adventure.

Of course, I don't want to come across as the high-strung, unrelaxed party pooper—a harsh label I've internalized over the years, long before I knew I was autistic. So instead, I fall into a familiar cycle: I make socially acceptable excuses instead of simply saying, "That's too last-minute for me." Or I get quietly frustrated and disappear. Or I push myself to follow through with plans that bring me serious stress.

If you ask someone who only knows the masked version of me, they'd probably say I'm easygoing and calm—but more often than not, that "easygoing" exterior is really me shutting down. It's what happens when I've reached a level of stress so high that I don't have the energy to process or respond, so I retreat inward and go quiet. Over time, pretending to be someone I'm not becomes so exhausting that the relationship quietly dissolves.

I mentioned earlier that I prefer short, simple outings over all-day events. That's largely because I get worn out more quickly than a neurotypical person might. This likely ties back to executive functioning in a few ways.

One reason is that I have to work harder to maintain focus and filter sensory input (as I discussed in a previous chapter). Being fully present with another person for a long time takes both mental and physical energy because unlike a neurotypical person, I have to actively monitor things like how much eye contact I'm giving, how much I am contributing vs. just listening, if I'm asking the right questions, and so on.

Since becoming a mom, this has only intensified. I'm constantly dividing my attention between managing my kids and trying to stay engaged in conversation. After just a couple of hours, I feel like I need to crawl into a dark cave and take a nap.

Another layer to this is the combination of task initiation difficulties and my tendency toward inflexibility. I am affected by the curse of wanting to cancel everything at the last minute because when the day comes that I need to venture out and do something different, my brain fights me about it.

I mentioned earlier how, even as a kid, I would automatically reject my mom's suggestions to go somewhere fun, like the zoo or the park. The same is still true. I rarely feel a burning desire to go take part in plans with friends during the lead-up to them, but when I make myself go, I usually come home happy. Tired, yes, but also recharged by real connection, assuming I felt safe to be myself with that person. It's not that I don't want to connect. It's just that I have to move through resistance to get there.

***

Helping Your Autistic Self

Looking back on my childhood and young adult life, I can clearly see the moments when I allowed my true self to show—and the people who made it feel safe to do so. Those moments stand out because they felt lighter, freer, more me. It's obvious now that I'm happiest when I don't have to pretend.

So, if you're an autistic person navigating friendships or the unmasking journey, here's what I want you to do: seek out the people who see and accept you as you are, and let go of the ones who don't. It may take more time for us to find the people worth keeping, but when we do, it makes for a much fuller and more peaceful life. Being honest about what you need and what doesn't work for you will also make socializing feel a lot less draining, and more enjoyable, in the long run.

To say that unmasking is easy would be a total lie. I still do it much of the time (at least to a certain extent), but I'm working on it little by little. To make this process a little less intimidating, start with letting in one person at a time.

For me, that person was Jade. At the time that I met her, I had nothing to lose except a person that I barely knew. But it turned out that gently allowing my authentic voice to be heard resulted in a friendship that means a whole lot to me.

The Diagnosis

Is it actually possible that I could be autistic?

It's the question that is the start of everything. The question that leads to more questions. That sends you into a spiral of research—lasting weeks, months, sometimes years. That pulls you back through every childhood memory you can possibly recall, holding each up to the light to examine, one by one.

The moment you start realizing that you are autistic upturns a hope that sat dormant, deep down inside you, for your entire life. You may feel a sense of new compassion for your younger self, a need to come running to the child within and hold them tightly.

You may wish you didn't try so hard to fit in. You may understand why you burned out so quickly while the rest of the world seemed to keep running the race.

All the while, you might feel elated—the fog is finally clearing. Everything makes sense for the very first time.

Perhaps you're wondering what specifically led me down the path to diagnosis, or even why I felt that I needed one.

Until I began my work with autistic individuals, my understanding of autism was limited to the same narrow, stereotypical representations most people know. Sadly, much of the world is still stuck there too—which is part of what inspired me to write this book.

As I continued my psychology career and started seeking out more information on my own, I began noticing subtle traits in myself. But at the time, all I had to compare them to was the clinical language of the DSM-V. Without diverse, lived experiences to draw from, it just wasn't enough to make anything truly click. I couldn't yet say, "Oh yeah, this is totally me."

Before I fully understood autism, I went through a phase of half-joking that I was "a little autistic"—usually when I missed a social cue, couldn't keep a conversation going, or got overly specific about plans. It didn't mean much at the time, but I think somewhere in the back of my mind I wondered: *Am I?*

Eventually, I was assigned to work with a teenage girl as a behavior therapist at my job. She was described as having lower support needs but struggled with things like executive functioning, impulse control, internet safety, and navigating relationships.

I'll admit, after working mostly with toddlers and young children up to that point, I was intimidated. Teenagers in general are scary—talk about indirect communication.

When I first met Haley and her mom, I felt immediate relief—they were both warm, friendly, and quick to welcome me into their home. I love when first meetings are open like that; it gives me a clearer sense of who a family is and how best to communicate with them. Some families are more reserved, hesitant to share challenges. Others get right to the heart of things. Haley's mom was desperate for some support—and got straight to the point.

We talked about potential therapy goals as well as the obstacles that had gotten in the way before. We discussed Haley's interests and what might motivate her as we worked on building good habits. Eventually, we narrowed our focus to improving skills like personal organization, task initiation, and independence with school-related responsibilities. We also wanted to support her in developing more positive relationships with both parents and peers.

After just a couple of weeks working with Haley and getting to know her, I actually started to question her diagnosis of autism. She was so different from the other kids that I had worked with, and different from adults on the spectrum that I have encountered. In fact, she sort of reminded me of myself when I was a teenager.

Haley was not a fan of being told what to do and did not respond well to incessant reminders from her mom when she put off important tasks. While that can seem like typical teenage behavior, her resistance reminded me of the PDA profile I described earlier—a persistent drive for autonomy that makes demands feel threatening, creating an anxiety-fueled sort of defiance.[1] The more pressure she felt, the more avoidant she became.

When I was younger, I showed some of these same tendencies, though more directly than I do now. If I was about to start my homework or clean my room and my mom came in to tell me to do it, I'd instantly lose all motivation. I wanted to do things because I decided to, not because someone told me to. As an adult, I don't usually have people hanging demands over my head, but I do notice that I can have pretty strong reactions to a lack of control when it comes to planning, people overstepping boundaries, or being given unsolicited advice.

Another way I related to Haley's experience was through our shared struggles with task initiation and approaching larger responsibilities, like end-of-semester projects, in linear, step-by-step ways. I grew up constantly putting off anything that didn't feel inherently satisfying—anything that didn't give me that little rush of dopamine, the brain's feel-good chemical released when we do something pleasurable, like eating, shopping, or achieving a goal.[2]

Haley, who had a dual diagnosis of both autism and ADHD, was also a dopamine chaser. She didn't get a big thrill from completing mundane tasks, and I could completely relate to her lack of motivation to study or stay organized. In fact, I still can today.

The difference is that now, as an adult, I've developed strategies using behavioral science to help make these tasks more tolerable. For example, I often won't let myself dive into a fun hobby until I've knocked out a few responsibilities first. It's a small system, but it works. Like Haley, I grew up hearing things like, "You're smart, you just don't apply yourself," from my mom, who was constantly trying to get me to stay on track.

When executive dysfunction meets demand avoidance, parent-child relationship conflict can seem almost inevitable.

On one hand, it's unreasonable to expect a parent to stand by while their child falls behind, scrolling through their phone instead of studying. But on the other, it's equally unrealistic to expect a child who instinctively resists demands to simply listen and decide to try harder.

In hindsight, I can see just how much tension I brought into my relationship with my mom during a particularly turbulent chapter of my life. Puberty hit hard, and the hormonal chaos completely derailed me—something I now know is not uncommon for autistic girls, who often experience heightened sensitivity to hormonal shifts. At the same time, I had started to feel "grown," but still didn't have real control over my decisions because, well, I was still a kid.

Because of my own difficulties with all of these things as a teen, I remember watching Haley and her mom interact (and regularly bicker) and thinking, *Wow, sounds just like my mom and me.*

At the time, the thought that I could be autistic hadn't even crossed my mind. I didn't yet understand how autism can look in girls or in other less-studied presentations. I had no concept of how vast and varied the spectrum really is.

So instead of questioning whether my own life experiences were atypical, I questioned whether Haley's diagnosis was accurate. Later down the road, I finally understood.

So when did I go from making autism jokes about myself to realizing the actual joke was on me? The turning point came shortly after I had my first baby. My world flipped upside down, and I was suddenly face-to-face with how poorly I handle change. My sensory sensitivities intensified, and tasks I once managed with ease now felt impossible.

Before motherhood, I had operated well within my own pace and carefully structured environment. But now, I couldn't keep up. My regenerative "me time" vanished—at least in those early months. I had expected new challenges, of course, but I hadn't expected to cope so badly with them. I hadn't yet understood just how essential quiet, solitude, and routine were for me. I had always assumed I was just like everybody else.

Realizing that my sensory sensitivities had been mistaken for depression and irritability was one of the biggest clues that I wasn't experiencing classic postpartum depression—but rather, at least to some degree, autistic burnout.

"I've always been bothered by certain sounds, but why does it feel so much more intense lately?" I remember asking my husband. It's because my body was in such a high state of stress that things became amplified. It felt hauntingly similar to the period of burnout that I had previously experienced in college.

Some time around then, I came face to face with the possibility, *What if I am actually autistic?* I revisited the diagnostic criteria again, not totally convinced, but suspicious. That's when my TikTok algorithm started doing its thing by providing me with an influx of video clips made by autistics who actually appeared to be a lot like me.

Most of these clips offered insight into how everyday life feels from an autistic perspective. I had no idea such a social media community even existed. I quickly got pulled in, scrolling through hundreds of videos, amazed at how deeply I related to what I was hearing.

I listened to these content creators share their deep, internal thoughts—speaking on topics like growing up undiagnosed, navigating specific social circumstances, the unique ways in which they think, special interests, sensory challenges, and so much more. I actually felt seen and understood by other people—a feeling that, for a very, very long time, felt foreign to me.

Like so many obsessively curious autistics out there, I needed to dig deeper. I needed to research—endlessly. So that's just what I did.

At that point, I began a year-long obsession with knowing all there is to know about autism, across a variety of demographic categories. Of course, I wanted to focus on autism in females with relatively low support needs (a term we use now in place of "high functioning"), since I felt that I fit best into this group.

I paired my research with allowing myself to join the online autistic community, more so as a fly on the wall than as a contributor. I wanted to hear personal stories, absorb anecdotal accounts, and get a deeper sense of whether I truly belonged.

At some point during this process, I took a few autism self-assessment screenings on my own, including the Autism Spectrum Quotient (AQ), the Ritvo Autism Asperger Diagnostic Scale–Revised (RAADS-R), and the Camouflaging Autistic Traits Questionnaire (CAT-Q).[3] Each one pointed strongly toward autism.

By the time several months of heavy research and self-examination had passed by, I was pretty sure that I would get a diagnosis in the event that I were to go through with a formal evaluation. Still, I kept telling myself that I didn't need an official diagnosis to validate what I had discovered—I could just assume that I was autistic and use the same tools that others in the community used to navigate the world more easily.

I tried to move on, identifying as "self-diagnosed" in my own mind. But I couldn't move forward—I didn't trust myself enough to stop questioning. I'd have a good day filled with smooth, fulfilling social interactions and suddenly think, *Nah, I can't be autistic.* I'd have a productive week and dismiss all the times it was nearly impossible just to get off the couch and start a simple task. Executive dysfunction who?!

This was always followed by a stretch of time outside my carefully curated environment, where everything would fall apart—a vicious cycle. Looking back, I can clearly see how black-and-white my thinking was. (Surprise! That's another autistic trait.) In reality, everyone has good days and bad days. Having a good day doesn't make me less autistic, and when a neurotypical has a bad day, it doesn't mean they are no longer neurotypical.

This truth also led me to reflect on something deeper: my own internalized ableism. What do I mean by ableism? It's the conscious or unconscious discrimination or prejudice against people with disabilities.[4] And yes—even people with disabilities can internalize these beliefs, especially if they've grown up in a culture that links the word disabled with shame, limitation, or brokenness.

The simple truth is that autistic people are allowed to be happy—they *should* be happy. In fact, under supportive and accommodating conditions, many would feel just as relaxed and content as anyone else. Much of our struggle comes not from being autistic, but from the constant effort to "fit into" a world that just doesn't mesh with our brain type. A world that is loud, fast paced, and built upon often trivial and exhausting social norms.

It took time for me to accept this idea that autistic people don't have to feel alien all of the time, that they don't have to look or even seem much different on the surface, and that they, frankly, can be female—and can be successful, pretty, admirable, a spouse, a mother, a business person, or whatever the heck else they want to be.

At the same time, that same admirable, successful person can also be the one who melts down behind closed doors, who appears calm on the outside but ruminates and feels out of control on the inside, who cannot stand to deviate from their rigid systems, who forces eye contact but doesn't like it one bit. All of that can exist in one person. And that person is still fully, authentically autistic.

The more that I came to terms with this, the more I wanted to seek out an official diagnosis to confirm all that I had learned about myself. But I had no idea where to start. I began by searching around and asking other female autistics who were part of online communities how they went about the process.

The first thing that I learned about adult autism evaluations was that they can be quite expensive and are not often covered by insurance (though this can vary by location and insurance type). This made me wonder if it would be worth it for me, especially since I was seeking diagnosis more for validation than for specific benefits or accommodations.

I put the idea aside for a while, or at least I tried to. At that point in my life, I was noticing new connections every single day—traits, reactions, or habits I'd either misunderstood or mislabeled for years. Things I'd once seen as flaws, or even positive traits I hadn't recognized as uniquely me, suddenly made sense through the lens of autism.

I began to see my identity in a new light. And that shift brought with it something I had struggled to feel for a long time: self-compassion.

I don't have a straightforward reason for feeling the need to hear a professional tell me that I was right. Perhaps it was true self doubt. Perhaps it was the autistic need to simply know. While I don't believe that every person should need external confirmation in order to identify as neurodivergent—or to use the tools that work well for us—for me, it was the only thing that stopped the wondering.

Naturally, when I came across a practice that was affordable, reputable, and specialized in the research and diagnosis of autism in the female phenotype, I jumped on the opportunity to be evaluated. It just made sense.

Part of the evaluation required me to write a lengthy narrative about my life, from childhood to present day, highlighting both my struggles and successes. I also had to complete several autism screening tools that were sent to me beforehand, some of which I had already taken on my own. The in-person portion of the evaluation involved answering more questions, drawn from a few different additional diagnostic tools. This process took a few hours to complete.

What I didn't realize was that the evaluators were also looking at small things such as my body language, mannerisms, and how I answered questions—considerations such as needing more processing time, asking clarifying questions, tangential thinking, etc.

Reading the extensive diagnostic report that followed revealed tendencies that I didn't even notice in myself, like looking away from my conversation partner while I speak, needing extra time to think before answering, or a subtle awkwardness in social exchanges that I had long assumed was just "me being me."

Overall, going through the diagnostic process felt very positive for me. But I know that's not the case for every woman—or for everyone with a less typical presentation. I've heard countless stories of evaluations that felt disappointing, infantilizing, or even invalidating. Sometimes the evaluator is simply outdated and lacks an understanding of how autism presents in females or across diverse gender identities. Other times, they fail to recognize or account for masking. They might assume that if someone can make eye contact or has friends, they don't meet the criteria.

Part of the problem is that autism is, at its core, an internal experience. It's not a visible condition like a broken bone or a rash that can be diagnosed with certainty. The external behaviors associated with autism simply stand as evidence of this internal experience.

But when an autistic person spends a lifetime learning how to appear more neurotypical—whether through direct instruction (look people in the eyes, hug your relatives), social pressure, bullying, or just watching and mimicking peers who seem to "fit in"—those observable signs can be hidden. Even if the person appears calm and socially competent on the outside, they may still be anxious, overstimulated, or completely dysregulated on the inside from the sheer effort it takes to mask.

I consider myself lucky to have felt so validated during my evaluation, and I genuinely hope others like me have similar experiences. The greatest gift I received wasn't just a diagnosis—it was a transformed sense of identity. And I'm not talking about a hollow, "Yes! I've got a label!" celebration. I'm talking about a deep, "Finally—I understand myself, and I can start giving myself the support I deserve" realization.

Not many people, especially outside the neurodivergent community, talk about the positives of receiving a diagnosis. As a society, something about labels tends to carry a negative connotation. And while it can be harmful to overidentify with certain labels, learning about oneself is usually a very healing process.

Unlike illnesses or mental health conditions that can often be treated or cured, a neurotype—like autism or ADHD—isn't something you "fix." It's an explanation of how a brain is wired and how it functions. And despite what some still believe, you don't grow out of autism. It shapes the way I think, how I process the world, and what I'm drawn to. It always has.

My autistic brain is why I'm so detail-oriented. It's why I get stuck in thought loops. It's behind my exceptional memory, my inability to lie convincingly, my love of rules, my intense emotions, and my passion for learning.

Would I want to "cure" it, if that were an option? In my darkest moments, I've entertained the thought. But when I look at the whole picture, the entirety of who I am, I'd say no. Because truthfully? This brain has taken me places I never would've gone otherwise.

Freefalling: The Terror and Freedom of Being Seen

So if getting a diagnosis was done solely for the purpose of confirming my suspicions, what was my next step? Just moving on with my life, or what?

Knowing is really only the beginning. Whether that knowing comes from a formal diagnosis or personal realization, it often sparks a series of emotional phases—many times followed by a deep call to action. Everyone's response is different. Childhood experiences, family dynamics, and the presence or absence of trauma all shape how such a life-altering revelation is processed.

For me, the feelings that followed my diagnosis went something like this:

Relief. As you can imagine, spending about a year's time analyzing your own existence, digging through research, and searching for answers feels like *a lot*. While I thoroughly enjoyed this exploration since I did learn so much, I almost think that I would have been disappointed to then find out that I was wrong about it all.

The further along I got, the more I felt at peace. Knowing that there was a real, neurological reason for why I struggled with certain things that others found easy—and even why I excelled at some things that others found difficult—caused me to appreciate and accept myself more than I ever had before.

Grief. Learning that the person you've been striving to be on the outside for years and years is not actually the real you sort of makes you resent the masked version of yourself. It also instills a deep desire to make amends with your inner child—the one that was too quiet, too dramatic, too obsessive, too afraid.

I was lucky to receive a lot of love from my family as a young child. Not everyone in my situation did. Yet as I grew from a little girl into a teen and social dynamics changed—kids got meaner, expectations were put in place, friend groups formed—that was when I felt I needed to hide parts of myself in order to be accepted.

All kids do this to an extent. It's the nature of wanting to be "cool" and fit in. I think the difference for me is that deep down, I didn't really get the thrill of doing the things that everyone else did, but I felt that I was supposed to. I didn't enjoy the conversations that most of my peers had, I didn't care for gossip, and I didn't feel the need to belong to a group. I was happy to just do my own thing, yet I felt that being a loner meant that there was something wrong with me.

Even now, I find myself in similar paradoxes—standing alone at a party, at peace with just watching the crowd, yet still worrying that others are assuming I'm uncomfortable, awkward, or rude. It's that push and pull between societal expectations and personal preference. It's the same reason I am always sure to plaster on a smile and be expressive, even though my face just wants to relax.

This grief stage was essentially my realization that I had put needless effort into doing things that weren't true to myself for far too long.

It was also grief for the times when I needed proper support, but didn't have any. While I managed well much of the time, I went through periods of extreme emotional dysregulation that were blamed on hormones and typical teenage rebellion. Because I was no longer a young child, I was expected to be able to be better at controlling my feelings and managing conflicts. When I could not, I was labeled as dramatic, sensitive, and difficult.

I now recognize these moments for what they were: autistic meltdowns—explosive full-body responses to a cognitive load that had simply become too much to manage.

The hardest part for both me and my family was that none of us had the context to make sense of what was happening. We didn't understand that my brain was wired to feel every-thing—emotions, sensations, and the world around me—with such intensity that it could easily become overwhelming. Had we known, the responses may have looked different, perhaps more gentle, more compassionate, and more compatible with my design.

A call to action. After moving through relief and grief, I realized that I wanted more than just understanding. I wanted to fully reconnect with my authentic self, the person who was hiding beneath the mask.

I had learned that the long-term effects of masking were detrimental to mental health and life satisfaction.[1] I remember my assessors remarking on how strikingly high my masking score was on the CAT-Q screening, which meant I had done quite a lot of pretending over the years—and it had likely been wearing on me.[2]

I decided it was no longer worth it to keep pretending. I was tired of over-analyzing every social interaction, of forcing myself to be uncomfortable, of trying so hard to seem "normal."

At first, I thought it would be simple—just stop caring what people think and start being myself. Easy, right? Like I could just reach into my back pocket, grab all the unnecessary worries I'd carried over the years, toss them into the air, and walk away, never looking back.

Unmasking is a slow, painful, one-step-forward-two-steps-back process. It's just not linear. Sometimes it's as simple as making minor accommodations for myself, but other times it's a tangled mess of attempts at honesty that just don't align with social expectations.

One of my biggest fears in unmasking was how it would be perceived by those who knew the masked version of me so well. I worried they'd think I was suddenly acting "more autistic" on purpose—or that I had let a disability label interrupt the version of myself they had come to accept as successful.

But just because I didn't let my autistic traits show on the outside doesn't mean they didn't exist beneath the surface.

People don't see me have meltdowns, because I don't usually let them happen in public (though I've definitely run to a bathroom to freak out on more than one occasion). People don't always see me fidget or stim, because I do it discreetly. They don't know that soft hugs feel awful to me, because I was taught from a young age that hugging is how you show you care.

Sometimes I force myself to maintain eye contact, even though it can send me into a state of panic—it just feels too intense. People don't know that I'm feeling that way.

They also don't know that I'm constantly monitoring my facial expressions and body language, making sure they match the situation. Or that I'm often secretly dying to ramble on about my special interests while everyone else is chatting about the weather or the latest movie.

People can't tell that I'm often exhausted or overstimulated after just a couple of hours at a noisy social event. When I go quiet in a group conversation, it's not always shyness—sometimes I just can't tell if what I want to say is going to come across as rude, intrusive, or weird. So I say nothing at all, because the fear of saying the wrong thing wins.

People just don't know that.

When I first started trying to unmask, a little bit at a time, I made more mistakes than I ever imagined I would.

Once, at the dinner table with my in-laws, I tried to follow through on something I'd recently committed to: breaking my habit of mentally editing everything I said, so I could speak more freely and authentically.

And that's when I blurted out that I hate New Year's Eve.

It wasn't just an offhand remark about the holiday itself. They were talking about their big annual New Year's celebration—the one they host every year and that we had always attended. I had essentially just admitted, to their faces, that I hated their party.

The minute that it slipped out of my mouth, I felt petrified. "I did not mean to say that out loud," I said quickly. I tried to explain how the noise and the music and the socializing was just a lot for me, but that it wasn't their fault. I could barely get the words out before I started crying uncontrollably and melting down.

I thought about it every day for weeks afterward, reliving the embarrassment over and over. I don't know if it was actually taken as badly as I feared—but God, it sucked.

That's when I realized unmasking wouldn't be anything close to easy. Not like I had thought.

Moving forward, I crawled back into my shell a bit, then slowly re-emerged—with a new awareness: I didn't actually know how to lose the social filter without coming off as rude. And maybe that's why it had been there in the first place.

For a while, I kept making mistakes. I still do sometimes.

For example, when I decided to be more open about my sensory sensitivities, my approach wasn't exactly graceful. I would wait until I was completely overloaded and irritated, then make some rash remark about "all the noise" before storming off for a break.

It was like I wanted to go full force with unmasking, but I had no idea how to do it without coming off as blunt, erratic, or just a little *too* brutally honest.

I still don't have unmasking figured out. It's something I struggle with daily—whether it's knowing who I can be open around, how much to reveal, or how to express myself without sounding rude.

The truth is, we *all* filter ourselves to some degree, neurotypes aside. We don't usually tell someone when their hair cut looks awful or when their home-cooked meal tastes bland. At work, we smile at customers even when we're having a terrible day, because that's part of the role we're expected to play.

That's what makes unmasking so complicated. It's not just a matter of letting everything go, but rather a process—of untangling who you are from who you thought you were, and of taking small, bold steps towards authenticity. And while stepping out, still taking care to protect the most vulnerable parts of yourself.

My mistake was neglecting to see the gray area, as I often do.

Throughout this process, I've learned that there are times to hold back, and doing so doesn't mean that I'm faking who I am. It just means that I'm protecting myself—or other people—from unnecessary hurt.

Masking for prolonged periods of time is extremely emotionally taxing, but unmasking takes its own toll, too.

One reason for this is that we are often learning who we are at the same time others are. I've been masking since I was young, so before I could even begin to live more authentically while being perceived by others, I first needed to untangle my true identity in private.

After spending a long time trying my very best to blend in, my mask and I became intertwined—and the border between who I tried to be and who I really was had faded almost completely.

For example, I thought I had adapted to challenges like sensory overwhelm. But what really happened was that I learned to suppress my needs—I ignored my body's signals in order to get by without accommodations. That's why I had spent so long confusing sensory overload with mood swings, and the need to stim with being short-tempered or easily annoyed.

I had spent so long ignoring my body's signals—to move, to withdraw, to pause and self-regulate—that pushing through became second nature. I assumed that was what everyone else did too, until I began to understand that my nervous system doesn't work like everyone else's.

Did I always keep a smile on because I meant it, or was it something I did so people would like me? Did I go to parties, proms, and get-togethers because I wanted to, or because I believed that was what I was supposed to do to fit in? Was I agreeable because that's who I was, or because I was afraid of being seen as difficult or "stuck in my ways"? Was I really me in those social interactions, or was I just mirroring the person I was talking to, hoping they'd enjoy my company?

Before I could feel free to be myself around others, I had to learn who I actually was—and what I truly needed.

Another nuance of unmasking is how deeply vulnerable it makes you. Being open about your neurodivergence automatically invites judgment, preexisting assumptions, and sometimes even disbelief. Unmasking all at once can feel jarring, for everyone involved.

You might start hearing things like:

"You never struggled with this before. Why now?"

"You've gotten by just fine up until now, and suddenly you need all these accommodations?"

"Well, you don't look autistic to me."

On the flip side, you may be met with reassurance—at least at first.

Often, the cycle looks something like this:

The autistic person opens up about being autistic. The neurotypical responds with well-meaning promises: "I'll always accept you." "It's safe to be yourself around me."

The autistic person takes this at face value and begins to unmask. Maybe they stop forcing eye contact. Maybe they stim more openly. Maybe they begin to speak up about their needs: "Can we turn the music down?"

But then the neurotypical becomes uncomfortable. The stimming seems strange. The request feels inconvenient. The shift in behavior doesn't match the version of the person they thought they knew.

Before long, the dynamic changes. The questions start. The doubt creeps in. The acceptance starts to feel conditional.

Sometimes leaving the mask on is a decision that we make, consciously or subconsciously, in order to protect our own energy. It would be a lie to say that I don't care at all about my ego. I'm working on caring less, but deep down, people's opinions still matter to me—enough to cause real emotional harm if I'm treated with stigma or dismissal.

And sometimes, the decision to stay masked isn't about emotional protection at all. Sometimes it's about physical or financial safety. No matter how capable you are, once people know you have a disability, they often treat you differently—whether subtly or overtly.

In the workplace, unmasking might mean asking for accommodations—a quieter space, more frequent breaks, or environmental adjustments—which, in certain environments, can be misinterpreted as signs that you're difficult to manage or need too much support.

The fact that some autistic individuals face this kind of discrimination is especially unfortunate, because autistics often bring valuable strengths to the workplace—like attention to detail, deep focus, loyalty, passion, and creativity. But when those strengths come alongside needs that don't align with neurotypical norms, they're often overlooked or dismissed.

So how could unmasking be physically harmful? In certain contexts, autistic traits or behaviors may be misinterpreted as aggressive, unstable, or rude. Some autistic people have intense reactions to unfamiliar environments or overwhelming sensory input—responses that can make others uncomfortable or even defensive.

As you can see, unmasking is so much more than a one-time decision. It's an ongoing process that changes daily, based on capabilities, safety, and circumstance. This is a concept that took me a while to grasp, and until I did, I felt like I was failing based on the moments when I returned to the mask because it felt safe and familiar.

But making moment-to-moment decisions about which parts of yourself to reveal and which to keep private is *completely okay*. In fact, it's responsible. You're simply honoring your own well being, and that matters more than meeting some made-up standard of what authenticity should look like.

While you're on this journey, the most important thing to prioritize is self-compassion. Unmasking is messy. Mistakes will happen. And it's in those moments that you'll be most tempted to turn against yourself—maybe even give up. But giving in to the voice of doubt and shame only pulls you deeper into the habit of hiding.

Embracing a truer identity, especially one that the world isn't used to, is an act of bravery. But even more importantly, it's a huge step towards the path to freedom.

Nothing that requires courage feels easy, but the reward is huge: being able to show up as unapologetically, fully *you*.

***

Helping Yourself

While unmasking will look different for everyone, here is what has helped me in my journey so far.

- **One step at a time.** Building the masked version of yourself took many, many years, so breaking down those walls cannot happen instantaneously. Give yourself time and grace. I learned that I had to spend some time in self-examination to first identify what felt inauthentic, why I was feeling fearful of releasing that part of me, and how I would act differently if I were in my own private space. From there, I started with small goals. For example, I'd let myself take a break from a noisy environment without worrying what others thought. Or I'd use a fidget item in public—something I once would have hidden.

- **Build a community of safe people.** Where you begin unmasking matters. If you're in an environment full of negativity or rejection, it can reinforce the urge to retreat behind the mask. Start by opening up to people who seem accepting and supportive. It's just a way of taking baby steps. One helpful strategy is to try being your authentic self in a brand-new relationship, where the stakes are low. *If this person doesn't vibe with me, I haven't lost anything deep. But if they do... I've gained* *someone I can be myself around.* I did this with a new friendship I made after my diagnosis, and it was freeing from the start. Why waste energy worrying about how to impress someone who doesn't want to know the real you?

- **Be gentle on yourself.** When I begin taking steps like this that require courage, I like to think of my inner child and how I can best support her in a loving, gentle way. I was a shy little girl who needed to be pushed to speak up, open up, and enter new situations bravely. Unmasking feels very much the same way for me as an adult. I am still that same little girl, just with much more life experience under my belt. If I make a mistake by saying something inappropriate, or by failing to speak up when I should have, or by having an awkward, rocky social interaction, I try my best to be forgiving. If we hold grudges against our imperfect selves, we'll never be able to move forward.

Helping Your Autistic Loved One

The best thing you can do for an autistic loved one is exactly what you're doing right now: taking time to educate yourself and understand what the world feels like from their perspective. For that, I thank you—from the bottom of my heart.

The world is still deeply misinformed about autism and the challenges that come with it. A frank comment is often seen as rude. A passionate infodump is seen as strange. A need for space or solitude is interpreted as impolite or distant. But these are not flaws; they're expressions of how an autistic brain navigates the world. In the end, we're all just trying to be seen, understood, and accepted—and that starts with listening.

The Art of Movement

"Leave your arms alone!" scolded my mother, for what felt like the hundredth time that day. "You're going to scar yourself."

I heard the same thing every day, but I just couldn't stop. I knew my mom was just trying to help, but I'd always respond with irritation and proceed to leave the room so I could secretly indulge in my shameful habit in peace.

I spent years as a chronic skin picker. More specifically, I picked and scratched at the skin on my upper arms. I did it anytime I was sitting still, with nothing else to do with my hands. It always became more intense during periods of anxiety or high stress. At one point, it got so frequent that my arms were covered in blemishes. It was super embarrassing, but I just couldn't stop.

Though it was clearly a negative habit that led to self-esteem issues, there was still something inherently soothing and satisfying about doing it. That repetitive action somehow calmed me—and at times, even helped me to focus better.

What I didn't know was that my picking habit was actually a form of stimming—a repetitive behavior that helps an individual self-regulate.[1]

Classic examples of autistic stims include hand flapping, spinning, and toe-walking. But stimming is not unique to autistics—everyone does it sometimes. If you've ever bounced your leg in a waiting room, clicked your pen over and over, or tapped your fingers on the table during a long meeting, you've stimmed.

The difference is that autistics tend to engage in these repetitive behaviors more often and more intensely than neurotypicals. A neurotypical might stim once in a while, but an autistic person stims daily—and *needs* to do so in order to regulate.

Why is this the case? It may simply be more necessary for us because our senses are heightened. We don't experience the world dully—we hear more, smell more, feel more, and experience emotions at more extreme levels. Because of this, it's easy for our systems to get thrown off, which explains the constant need for self-soothing actions.

I realized that my skin-picking habit was actually a form of stimming after hearing stories from other autistic women who shared the same behavior. Just knowing I wasn't alone made me feel less ashamed.

It also got me thinking: how could I meet that same need for repetitive sensory input without causing lasting damage to my skin? I started experimenting with replacements—I bought a fidget cube and focused on keeping my hands busy in other ways. Eventually, I broke the habit for the most part.

By that point, I had also started to notice other stims I engaged in regularly. One in particular was bringing my hair to my face and rubbing it against my mouth and nose. It was such an unconscious habit that other people picked up on it before I did.

"Serena likes to smell her hair!" a coworker once playfully remarked.

Do I really do it that often? I wondered.

So I started tuning in to my own behaviors even more. I realized I rubbed my hair on my face every time I felt anxious. Both the smell and the sensation soothed me.

Like many autistics, I don't only stim when I'm stressed—I also do it when I'm overwhelmed with positive emotions. I might wave my hands excitedly when I feel pure joy. I might jump, sing, or dance, because when I feel happiness, I *embody* it. Even the best emotions can sometimes feel too big for my body.

Not all stims manifest as physical movements—some are verbal in nature. Repeating certain sounds, words, or phrases can also be regulating and enjoyable for autistics.

Echolalia, which refers to the repetition of language spoken by others, is a common autistic trait.[1] It can occur for different reasons, and making this distinction is especially important when it comes to supporting children with language delays who may be on the spectrum. In some cases, it's part of how spoken language is learned—particularly through something called gestalt language processing, where whole phrases are learned and repeated before being broken down into individual words.[2]

But echolalia can also act as a stim when the repeating of words or sounds, whether out loud or internally, simply feels soothing, grounding, or inherently satisfying.

Autistic people naturally tend to latch onto things—sounds, patterns, words—especially when they have a melodic or rhythmic quality. Some stim by counting aloud, reciting memorized lines, or repeating words or phrases that feel good rolling off the tongue, even if those words aren't used in a communicative way.

For example, a person might latch onto a nonsense word and repeat it randomly or rhythmically throughout the day. That's vocal stimming.

I do this too. I have a whole dictionary of meaningless words that I spout out randomly, often without realizing it. There's also a clear connection between how I'm feeling emotionally and how much I stim. The more intense the emotion, whether it's overwhelm or joy, the more repetition tends to show up.

Other forms of stimming can involve things like sights, sounds, textures, or smells—anything that helps regulate the nervous system or simply feels good enough to repeat. Sometimes it's about calming down, sometimes it's about expressing joy, and sometimes it's just because it feels *right*.

It's important to remember that stimming often begins in childhood, even if it looks different from how it might present in adults. Some of the most common forms of stimming in autistic kids include:

- Flapping their hands

- Shaking or rocking their head back and forth

- Jumping or bouncing in place

- Spinning themselves or objects

- Walking on tiptoes

- Looking at objects up close or out of the corners of their eyes

- Wiggling fingers in front of their face

- Repeating sounds, words, or phrases (echolalia)

- Rewinding and rewatching the same video clip repeatedly

- Lining up toys or objects in precise arrangements

- Mouthing or chewing on non-food items

It's also worth noting that many typically developing children may engage in some of these behaviors at one point or another. When considering whether a child might benefit from an autism evaluation, the key factor is frequency.

A child on the spectrum will typically stim much more often—and more intensely—than a neurotypical child. And of course, other core features of autism would need to be present to support a diagnosis.

Stimming behaviors also tend to shift and evolve as an autistic child grows into an autistic adult. After years of being told to "stop that" or "just sit still," many behaviors become suppressed, while others emerge in more subtle forms.

Autistics who are especially socially aware often find ways to stim discreetly or reserve those comforting repetitive movements for when they're alone, behind closed doors.

Some of my stims happen when I'm feeling happy, energized, or deeply relaxed. Others show up when I'm anxious, overwhelmed, or uncomfortable. Some I've done for as long as I can remember, and some I'm still rediscovering, after years of masking.

Here are some stims I use when I'm experiencing positive emotions or when I'm simply unwinding:

- Rubbing my feet together ("cricket feet"—the absolute best!)

- Rubbing a blanket or stuffed animal against my face

- Audibly sighing (a big, loud "Ahhhhhh" that sometimes startles my family because it sounds more like a yell)

- Singing

- Jumping

- Walking or bouncing on my tiptoes

And here are some stims that tend to come out when I'm feeling anxious, overwhelmed, or trying to self-regulate:

- Picking at my skin

- Cracking my knuckles

- Wiggling my fingers

- Playing with jewelry

- Twirling my hair

- Bringing my hair to my face and rubbing it against my lips or nose

- Jumping up and down

- Shaking or flapping my hands

Until recently, I didn't even notice that I was stimming. But now that I understand why we do it, I can easily connect the dots between my feelings and behaviors. I also now understand that some of my harmful behaviors—urges that I try to resist—are just my body's way of trying to regulate.

When I experience emotions that feel too big, I sometimes find myself digging my nails into my thighs, pulling at my hair, or on my worst days, hitting myself in the head. Not cool. I know.

Instead of continuing to suppress my feelings until they manifest as an explosion, I've been consciously trying out different stims that provide a safety valve of release for negative energy so that I don't reach my breaking point. One of these stims is hand flapping.

The first time that I let myself do it felt wildly uncomfortable. Fake. Embarrassing—even though I had done it in my own private space, where no one could see me or judge me. Somehow I felt like a fraud, wrongly taking up space that belonged to those with higher support needs. But I just wanted to know how it felt. What is it about hand flapping that often feels so good to autistic people?

So one day, when I felt the buzz of loud, messy, stinging energy in my body, I tried it. And it felt... good. Hmm. I get it.

Since that day, I understood that stimming is for *everyone*—and it doesn't matter what it looks like. Everyone stims. But autistics *need* to. If flapping my hands stops me from causing harm to my body, I'm going to do it—no justification needed.

In a way, I like to think of stimming as a practice of honoring the body—similar to how we view yoga or meditation. Stimming is different, though, in that it often happens without any conscious effort.

While that may be true for many people, high-masking autistics like myself sometimes have to consciously relearn how to tune into the body, follow its signals, and stop suppressing what it wants to do.

Leaning into this has given me an indispensable tool for regulation—something I can access anywhere, anytime. Over time, I've made gradual progress in recognizing the earliest signs that my nervous system is off: a racing heart, jitters, heat rising in my body, growing tension, and irritability.

That's when I pause—take some deep breaths, retreat to a calmer environment if I can, and let myself move in whatever way my body needs. Sometimes that means a quiet sigh and pressing my face against a soft blanket. Other times, it means screaming into a pillow and jumping wildly to release the tornado inside me.

Neurodiversity people often feel emotions more intensely—and more physically—than others. What might seem small to someone else can build in us and become overwhelming.

For me, sadness feels like death. Anger feels like fire. And happiness, over even the smallest of things, can feel like ecstasy bursting forth inside me.

For many of us, emotions are much more than mere thoughts. They take over our bodies. I often feel like I am in a constant state of reaching for the part of me that exists outside of my emotions, searching for my personal equilibrium, a calm balance that lies beyond the mess in my mind.

But finding it won't come from pushing feelings away. It comes from letting them move through without taking over, and learning how to respond instead of react. Sometimes that means moving. Sometimes it means resting. And sometimes it just means giving myself permission to feel without shame.

Unfixable: Lessons from Therapy

Upon receiving my diagnosis, there was an almost instantaneous sense of hope and direction for the future. To me, it felt as if I'd just solved a giant mystery—I finally had explanations for so many pieces of who I am that had made me feel estranged from other people my whole life. This meant that I was one step closer to true becoming.

I had tried therapy once in the past, when I was going through my period of extreme burnout in college—the one that resulted in a complete loss of functioning. At my very first session, I went in and explained that I was experiencing such debilitating anxiety that I had to essentially pause my life. My therapist, Elaine, then proceeded to go through the usual first session slew of questions in order to gather more information about me:

"Do you have any existing diagnoses?"

"Any history of trauma?"

"Have you ever been to therapy before?"

I sat across from her and answered succinctly, eager to get to the part where I magically learn how to obliterate my panic attacks forever, be okay again, and forget that time in my life ever happened.

Elaine was the first person to ever teach me about mindfulness, the practice of present moment awareness. Mindfulness means paying attention to your body and surroundings using your five senses, and it can be practiced anywhere, any time.

Basically, Elaine recommended that I start savoring everyday activities by staying more present in my body. I remember her specifically telling me that I might benefit from getting a fuzzy new pair of slippers and remembering to fully bring my attention to the way that they feel each time I slide my feet into them in the morning.

And while today, I am a huge believer in the wonders of mindfulness, at the time, I had simply reached a point where I needed much more. Even very effective self-care skills will fail in times of crisis, and that's where I was.

Seeing Elaine felt like dipping my toes into the world of therapy. I think just the idea of having some form of professional support felt more reassuring than the support itself. Ultimately, I didn't get much out of my first go at therapy and my mother and I warmly joke about the fuzzy slippers to this day.

I thought that I'd never try therapy again, but fast forward five years and a few autism suspicions later, I decided to revisit the idea.

I had two conditions for finding another therapist. First, they needed to be highly credentialed. Because my first experience had been underwhelming, I developed the (incorrect) belief that working with a PhD-level licensed psychologist was the only way to get quality care.

I assumed my mediocre first therapy experience was due to Elaine's limited credentials—I just needed someone more educated. But looking back, I now realize what I truly wanted: someone who could take a deep dive into my psyche, pick me apart, and finally help me make sense of my behaviors and inner world.

Eventually, I came to find out that the only person who could fully do that was me. While a therapist or psychologist can help lead you closer to those complex answers, those who exist outside of your mind and body can only search so far. The truth is that you can't count on a single person—not even the smartest person on the planet—to figure you out. That's just not how it works.

I decided it was important to me that my next therapist understood autism, at least to some degree. At this point in time, I was moving closer to uncovering my neurodivergence, but it was still just the beginning of my journey. I had yet to learn that the diagnostic process is not simple, nor is it a one size fits all. I assumed I could just find any psychologist, explain my concerns, and be told definitively whether or not autism was the answer.

So I scoured the internet, determined to find someone more knowledgeable than my previous therapist. I planned to bring up autism right away. More than anything, I wanted clarity. I needed to know who I was—for sure.

Enter therapist number two: Kat. The first thing she asked me to do was fill out an extensive intake form outlining what I was struggling with and what I hoped to gain from therapy.

I took my time with it. I explained my history with depression and anxiety—or at least, what I had labeled it at the time—and how overwhelmed I felt trying to meet the demands of life after having my son. I summarized the sensory processing challenges I was facing, noting how amplified they had become. And finally, I shared how I'd started connecting the dots between so many of my behaviors and experiences, leading me to suspect that I might be autistic.

"I am hoping to further explore the possibility that I may be on the autism spectrum," I wrote.

I hoped that she would believe me, but I feared she might assume I was just very mixed up—especially after meeting me and seeing that I was not only quite accomplished, but also well-spoken and intellectual. I've read countless stories from other autistics who were completely dismissed by professionals for those very reasons. Maybe, in my heart, I worried the same thing—that I wasn't autistic at all, just an imposter looking for something to blame.

So there I sat behind my computer screen, promptly ten minutes early for my first session, sweating bullets as my heart beat picked up faster and faster. I've always had a tendency to rehearse social scripts before interactions, using them as a way to self-soothe and feel prepared. I tried to imagine the kinds of questions she might ask and how I would explain what had brought me to this point. The question looped in my mind, over and over: Would she reject me?

Then she appeared on the screen. "Serena? Hello! Nice to finally meet you," she said, smiling and adjusting her glasses. Kat radiated warmth immediately, which gave my heartbeat the chance to begin slowing. I wriggled in my chair, pulling one leg up underneath the other, my usual awkward but comfortable sitting position.

To my surprise—and through sheer luck—my experience felt much more validating than I had expected. Immediately after discussing medical and mental health history, Kat cut right to the chase. "I saw that you have concerns about potential autism," she said. "Could you tell me some more about that?"

"Yes. I have wondered about autism for a while now, but I'm just beginning to take the thought seriously. You see, I've had sensory issues, social challenges, and problems with breaking routine my whole life, but after having my son, all of those things amplified to a whole other level!"

I had been especially confused by the way that these difficulties went from manageable to completely out of control. It was one of the reasons why I initially doubted that autism could be the cause—I told myself that it just had to be some sort of imbalance within my body, a hormonal shift or deficiency of some sort.

I was so convinced of this that I had seen a naturopathic doctor to get blood work and find out what was going on. My hormone levels came back normal. I was not largely deficient of anything. However, my cortisol levels were very high.

Cortisol is the body's main stress hormone, and while some cortisol is necessary for several important functions, too much can lead to a host of stress-related issues. It made sense that increased stress would elevate pre-existing challenges, but what I did not understand was the root cause of my stress: being an undiagnosed autistic, absent of effective coping strategies during a naturally busy season of life.

"I would like to go through a screening assessment with you that could help indicate whether or not you may meet criteria for autism, if you don't mind," Kat told me.

"Of course. That sounds good," I replied, trying my best to hide my excitement in getting another step closer to finding my truth. At that point, I had done every screening tool imaginable, but to have a professional willing to explore this with me felt much more real.

The Autism Spectrum Quotient (AQ) is a 50-question screening questionnaire that measures autistic traits in adults without intellectual disability.[1] Because this tool has strong validity and reliability, a score above the threshold likely indicates autism, though it cannot provide a diagnosis by itself.

My score not only surpassed the threshold, but it was right in line with the average among autistics, according to the research.

Ultimately, Kat told me it was reasonable to believe I might be on the spectrum, but that she couldn't provide an official diagnosis since we hadn't done a formal assessment. "I've worked with neurodivergent individuals before," she explained, "but it's not my area of expertise. There are therapists who specialize in that if it's something you want to pursue—but I'll also do my best to support you."

Just the simple act of freely and genuinely considering me a neurodivergent individual made me feel more seen than I ever had in my life. As I continued talking with Sharon, my wall of defense and fear began to soften—because, for once, it felt like someone truly believed me. Someone took me seriously, and I hadn't expected that at all.

Growing up in the '90s and 2000s, the world hadn't yet embraced the open acknowledgment of feelings, mental illness, or disabilities as just parts of life. These were seen as "yucky" things—taboo topics that weren't discussed openly. As a teen grappling with anxiety and low moods, I was encouraged to hide my struggles and push through, because I was supposed to be strong.

And while a little positivity and grit can be helpful, having the language to describe personal experiences is just as important. It helps reduce shame and build self-understanding. Alongside this, reducing stigma by talking more openly about mental health has helped people feel less alone—and has made space for communities to form, share what's worked, and support one another through what hasn't.

Millennials like myself were among the first generations to experience both the stigma-heavy era of mental health and the newer era of openness and normalization. That contrast helps explain why finally receiving a label for my unique life experience felt so fresh and exciting.

The words I used to describe myself before my diagnosis were far more damaging than simply acknowledging that I'm autistic.

Before, I was socially awkward. Now, I understand that my neurotype doesn't naturally pick up on social norms.

Before, I was obsessive. Now, I recognize my special interests and ability to hyperfocus.

Before, I was sensitive and dramatic. Now, I know I process more environmental input than most people do.

Before, I was lazy. Now, I understand I struggle with executive dysfunction because of how my brain is wired.

The list goes on.

Because I felt so seen and comfortable talking with Sharon, I decided to continue working with her for the time being. Since I had no clear idea where to start with pursuing a formal diagnosis, I figured I would explore that alongside traditional therapy.

Unfortunately, after just a couple of sessions, I found out that my insurance didn't cover any of our time. At the time, I was managing okay—not perfectly, but not in complete burnout. Since I could get by, I couldn't justify paying out of pocket, so I discontinued therapy.

I remember sending Kat an email to explain the situation, thanking her for our brief but positive work together, and for the resources she shared. She wished me well, and suddenly, I was alone again in my journey of self-discovery.

Months went by, and life continued to show me that it's like an ocean—always moving, shifting from high tide to low tide over and over again. I had days when I felt completely knocked down by the demands of navigating motherhood alongside my own internal world. But I also had days when I felt like I was truly thriving, almost enough to believe the illusion that I was going to have it all together and forget I ever thought something was amiss—that there was an undiscovered piece of me called autism that could explain everything all at once.

Still, the pull to know—to finally have an answer—kept tugging at me. My brain always wants to understand why. It craves problem-solving and finds comfort in having a logical explanation for everything in my world. Not knowing for sure whether autism could explain my challenges felt like a cliffhanger. From the moment I dipped my toes into the pool of research on neurodiversity, I was determined to dive in fully—and come back with a clear yes or no. I also believed that a formal diagnosis would lead to more personalized support tailored to my neurotype, potentially changing how therapy would work for me.

Knowing what I know now, I see how my thinking was too naive, too linear, too black-and-white. I don't regret my diagnosis by any means, but finding help that fits you perfectly—as an individual shaped by a lifetime of experiences, environmental influences, possible trauma, and a unique physiological make-up—is simply impossible. There will be bits that resonate, moments of grand epiphany, and still, advice that makes you want to curl up in a ball and whine about how "nobody gets it." I've experienced all of this.

When it comes to therapy, it's all about finding someone who feels like a good fit for you. After switching therapists a few times, I've realized it's a bit like dating—the more you discover what you don't want, the clearer it becomes what feels right.

My next therapist experience was one that felt so wrong. By this point, I had my formal diagnosis, understood myself better, and wanted more tailored support. I decided to specifically seek out a therapist who specialized in neurodivergence. I scrolled through dozens of profiles online, reading about their education, interests, approaches, and prior experience. I read client reviews to spot both their strengths and areas where people felt unsupported. From there, I compared and narrowed down therapists who had specific knowledge in the autism field.

Then I landed on Melanie.

In her bio, Melanie stated that she was a certified autism specialist with many years of experience working with both children and adults. She described herself as bubbly, positive, and motivating. "I want to empower you to live your best life. I'll be the wind beneath your wings!" she claimed.

The vibe I got from Melanie was free-spirited—and that was exactly what I'd always dreamed of being. I'm pretty sure there's a piece of that in me too, buried beneath my need for control, order, and predictability. I wanted that part to come out. And I began to think that maybe Melanie could inspire it, maybe even make it happen.

I was so ecstatic when I found Melanie's therapist profile. I was excited that she knew a lot about autism and I liked the persona that I saw. But in hindsight, I see that I had high hopes, and was setting myself up for a huge disappointment.

When Melanie's face popped up on the screen for our first session (because... virtual therapy from the comfort of your own home is such an autistic win), I instantly knew I'd been right about the kind of person she was. She appeared in an RV, embellished with plants hanging in the background. It was a warm summer day, the windows were open, and I could hear wind chimes gently clinking together in the breeze.

"I actually live off-grid and travel full-time," she explained.

Wow, I thought. I found myself a hippie therapist.

But it was so refreshing—so different—that I just wanted to know more about this mystery woman who seemed to hold the secret to a carefree and happy life. She radiated it.

"Tell me about you. Why are you in therapy?" She asked me.

I started by explaining that I had recently received an autism diagnosis and wanted to explore some lifelong challenges that seemed related.

Her expression shifted as I spoke. The warmth faded, replaced by a critical, questioning demeanor. "You got an autism diagnosis? Where? What kind of assessment did they use? Was it a full psychological evaluation or just an autism-specific screening?"

Suddenly, I was bombarded with questions about my evaluators, my behaviors, and why I'd chosen to get assessed at 29. It felt like an unexpected job interview—one I hadn't prepared for. I did my best to explain the personal challenges I believed autism helped make sense of, but she replied, "You're just so articulate. I'm really not seeing autism here."

My body filled with rage. I held back tears as she continued to question me, all before we had even begun to build any kind of safe, therapeutic connection. It felt like I had flipped a switch, and suddenly her sole mission was to prove she was right—that in just three minutes of conversation, she could definitively conclude I wasn't autistic, simply because I spoke well. Deep down, I knew I understood myself better than some stranger I'd just met, but despite that, I couldn't stop myself from feeling stupid. Once again, I was not being believed.

The likelihood of me wanting to see Melanie again at that point was next to nothing, but I tried to hold myself together and just see what sort of advice she might have for me. I promised myself not to use the word "autism" again—to just speak of my concerns organically. I had no desire to trigger whatever *that* was again.

I talked about my difficulties with opening up to other people and connecting beyond surface level, unless my very narrow range of interests were involved.

"Oh, so you have social anxiety!" she yipped, as if coming to some sort of impressive conclusion.

"Um... I don't really feel like I'm anxious around people all the time," I pushed back. "I just feel that it's hard to form relationships, and most of the time I don't care to, but I feel like I should."

"Ah, you need to start small. I'm going to give you an assignment for the week. Go to the store and just practice saying hi to people! Give people compliments, too! It's a great way to connect. I just love talking to people," she told me.

"Uh, yeah. I have no problem saying hi to people or giving compliments." I just didn't see the point of small talk—ugh.

The entire session felt like a cycle of me explaining my struggles, only for her to misinterpret and invalidate how I felt—because she was such a people person, convinced the whole world would be better off the same way. Needless to say, I left the session crying—overtaken by a mix of hurt, anger, and disappointment because things had gone completely opposite from what I expected. My next question was simple but heavy: Should I keep searching, or just give up?

After another few months of pouting about my horrible therapy experience, I went on the search again, this time refining my requirements to include: must be knowledgeable about not just autism, but nuanced presentations of autism among women and high-masking adults. Then, along came therapist number three.

Jane described her practice as a safe space for her clients to feel heard. *Okay, sounds good so far,* I thought as I read her profile.

Then she noted that she had lots of experience working with neurodivergent individuals. *Okay. Approaching with caution.*

I decided to reach out to Jane via message to try to get a better feel for what she knew. "Hello! I saw your therapist profile and feel like you may be a good fit for me right now. I was recently diagnosed with autism as an adult, and I was just wondering if you have experience working with autistic adults who present as more 'low support needs,'" I said.

I was happy to see her response, that seemed to affirm what I was hoping for. She wrote, "Hi Serena! Yes, I have lots of experience working with people on the spectrum! I am ADHD myself and have raised neurodivergent children of my own!" Thank goodness—she understood, for real.

After my first session with Jane, I came out of my office—not crying—and was washed over with relief at the fact that I was believed. She didn't question my diagnosis or act like she knew more about me than I did. She listened as I talked about struggles I'd faced for years, and she validated everything. I ended up working with her for quite some time, grateful to have finally felt understood. Yet after a while, I began to notice something about my therapy: I wasn't really getting anywhere.

Jane was kind, supportive, and authentic. Every time I presented with a problem, she was able to understand why I felt the way that I did. Sometimes she even shared stories about how she could relate as someone with ADHD.

The healing that came from talking to her was a necessary first step in getting support—I needed to be able to share about my experiences and have them taken for exactly what they were. I was never told to "push through," that I would eventually get over it, or that I was mixed up and misdiagnosed.

I needed practice speaking without the constant fear of judgment—a slow rewiring of neural pathways from what I'd grown used to. Still, I eventually realized that insight alone wasn't enough. I needed to take action in the areas of my life that felt especially challenging. It was then that I ended therapy with Jane—and found Liza.

And Liza was the real deal. At our very first session, I explained that I had just had my second baby and that my nervous system felt completely thrown off. The combination of physical healing from birth, trying to re-balance my hormones, and adjusting to a new baby and a new routine had sent me into a familiar, temporary state of fight or flight—even my blood pressure was elevated.

By that point, I knew the feeling well. There had been several times in my life when I felt "stuck" in hyperawareness—a constant surge of adrenaline pulsing through me (and not the kind you get from roller coasters). I just didn't know how to escape it. I had tried everything: supplements, meditation, exercise, benzodiazepines, SSRIs, CBD oil—you name it. But there came a point when my amygdala (the "lizard brain" responsible for activating fight-or-flight responses) became too powerful for those methods to work anymore.

While I was going through this, Liza introduced me to something called polyvagal theory, a framework in which we can learn to calm our body's nervous system through activation of the vagus nerve, a cranial nerve that helps to regulate several automatic bodily functions such as heart rate, blood pressure, and digestion.[2]

The more that I spoke with Liza and learned from her, the more I was able to see that many of my problems were stemming from emotional dysregulation caused by a nervous system that was impaired. Autistics naturally are incredibly sensitive to their environments because of brain differences. Because the world is filled with constant sensory input, it can take a toll on those of us who are wired to process everything more intensely. While neurotypicals push on, effectively filtering out the chaos around them, we take it all in—and thus, require more protection, tenderness, and compassion toward our minds and bodies.

The incorporation of somatic therapy, a type of therapy that focuses more on the body and how our feelings show up within it, has been much more helpful to me than talk therapy alone. While talking and processing is important, it only takes me so far. Real progress, for me, seemed to begin when I learned about how to allow emotions to show up without destroying me.

This was also when I realized that intense feelings cause me to act out of character, dulling my ability to speak my truth without hurting others. When I experience a strong emotion—whether triggered by something someone says or by an irrational thought that suddenly enters my mind—I no longer feel safe. I curl up inside that emotional state and stay there far too long. The world around me fades. Logic and reason slip away.

In those moments, all I care about is protecting myself—my overactive amygdala tries to convince me I'm under attack by a bear, when really, I just need to set a boundary, confront someone, or meet a need as simple as a few minutes of peace and quiet. Somatic therapy taught me that by learning to regulate my nervous system, I can lower those walls of defense and see things clearly again, allowing me to get my needs met in a calm, rational way.

Learning this stuff is not easy or quick. I'm still working on it, and I still fail regularly—usually in the form of an overstimulation outburst that no one saw coming, because I held it in until I couldn't anymore.

When it comes to other areas—like social dilemmas, interpersonal conflict, and self-management—therapy is a different story. When I bring a specific problem to discuss, it often feels less like I'm gaining new insight and more like I'm psychoanalyzing myself for an hour while someone quietly observes. I've stumped therapists more times than I can count by presenting both the issue and a fairly accurate analysis of it—only to be met with a long, uncomfortable pause.

I'm good at analysis of my own behaviors and incredibly self aware, for the most part. While I can easily figure out why I might have felt or acted a certain way, I have a much harder time figuring out how to "fix" things—and therapists haven't had much luck either. I could walk into a session with all the right words and all the right theories, but no idea how to make the things that I struggle with any easier to handle.

Am I just unfixable? I find myself wondering often. I'm aware of my mountains and my valleys. I can trace how those steep mountains were formed and why I find them so hard to climb. And yet, there's always some invisible blockade stopping me from making the climb any easier.

In some ways, I do think I'm unfixable—not because something is wrong with me, but because parts of who I am just don't blend with the way the world works. I was made for quiet spaces. Made for skipping the small talk and getting straight into the good stuff. I was made for deep focus, for learning, for unraveling patterns, for getting lost in details. I was made for structure and constancy. But the mismatch isn't me—it's the world I was dropped into. After years of trying to bend to fit the mold, I've come to the conclusion that I really am unfixable—but maybe it's because I don't need fixing.

The Quest for Self Compassion

March 31, 2023

Why is it so hard for me to function like a normal person? Every tiny detail feels like a full-blown crisis, and I'm so sick of my brain turning everything into something to obsess over. My head is a mess. It's cluttered, chaotic, and loud. I can't seem to slow anything down. I'm snappy, restless, worn thin by things that shouldn't take this much energy. What makes it worse is knowing I don't even have that much on my plate—not compared to most people. And yet, I still feel like I'm barely holding it together. I hate how easily I spiral, how quickly I lose my grip.

Lately, I just feel broken.

I wrote this journal entry when I was in the thick of mother-hood, working part-time remotely, and caring for my home all at the same time. The cover of the journal says, "Give yourself grace." In hindsight, I can see that I wasn't giving myself a single ounce of it.

Around this time in my life, I was functioning above my normal threshold. I had not yet discovered my neurodivergence and I was stuck in a loop of continually comparing my performance to those of other young moms who had even more on their plates than I did. I was not treating myself well by any means, but that didn't matter to me. All that mattered was that I felt different and therefore, inadequate.

I watched other women work full-time jobs, come home and cook meals, take care of their children, and clean the house late into the evening while still seeming to have the energy to do it all again the next day. I saw stay-at-home moms, like myself, who didn't seem to repeatedly lose their minds taking their kids to all those overstimulating play places.

Meanwhile, I was at the point where I could barely hold a conversation with another person in a crowded area without being completely overwhelmed and zapped of energy by the end of it. Because I was doing a lot more than I could easily handle, very simple things took a lot out of me.

Yet I didn't see the signs for what they were—indicators that I needed to accommodate myself and reduce my load. Instead, I viewed my shortcomings as gigantic personal failures. That mindset pulled me into a relentless cycle of negative self-talk, all without any real awareness of what was happening. It began with comparisons and gradually spiraled into ruthless self-examination—a quest to uncover every way I was different, and why each of those differences somehow meant I was wrong.

Something about the way that I saw myself changed at some point between youth and adulthood. I always felt different, but when I was younger, I took pride in my uniqueness. I felt creative, quirky, fun, free. Perhaps imposing these labels upon myself was how I coped with not fitting in with the people who seemed to be all the same. If I can't be liked for the person that I am, why not embrace the lone wolf persona and own it?

I recall moments when I wished that I understood the invisible social rule book that most others seemed to have. I wondered what it would have been like to be a part of a close group of friends. But an instant later, I'd think to myself, *Why would I want to be like them? How boring!* I simply had no interest in gossip, sports, fashion, or TV—the things that seemed to matter to them.

I gravitated to people who were similar to me, who liked the arts, strange humor, deep conversation, and random fun facts. Somehow, a part of me felt broken while another part of me felt strangely proud—like being different made me more interesting than people who all seemed the same. At that time in my life, I saw myself as superior in that sense.

But then I grew up. And at some point I got concerned with success. I believe that somewhere deep down, years and years of feeling out of place weighed on me. That was when I decided to get a fancy degree and a career that would both make me feel safe and prove that I was smart and capable.

When I told people that I was studying to be an accountant, they would always remark about how they could "never do that" and how I must be really good at math (I am not, but it's actually a misconception that accountants need to be good at math). I felt that focusing on my career was what I needed to do to feel fulfilled in the success department. Of course, that's when it all came crashing down and my personal rock bottom opened my eyes to the fact that I was miserable. Thank God.

I would have never imagined that my version of success would be redefined as working in human services, becoming an autism advocate, and publicly sharing a diagnosis I didn't even know I had for most of my life—but here I am.

I even wrote a book! And while that might be seen as an impressive accomplishment, I'll admit—humbly and honestly—that I still wrestle with serious self-criticism nearly every single day.

Before my diagnosis, I was "dramatic, too sensitive, too stiff, stubborn, antisocial, self-centered"—and so many other things. After 29 years of identifying with those harmful labels, I was suddenly given an explanation that made everything finally make sense.

I know who I am now. The problem is, the world still doesn't.

I'm incredibly grateful to have a new lens through which to see my differences—but I still catch myself flipping back to the old one, imagining how I must look through the eyes of people who don't understand me. Cue the voices of the past—mine and others'—the ones that created those labels in the first place.

Only recently have I come to the realization that the end of my suffering begins when I stop trying so hard to be understood—and instead start living in alignment with the voice of self-compassion. Here are some small steps I've taken to move in that direction:

- **Journaling.** I now have a place to dump all of my thoughts—both the ones I have about myself and the ones I imagine other people might have about me. This helps in two big ways. First, it turns a rumination (a thought loop) into something tangible. Once it's written down, I find it a little easier to let go of. Second, it helps me process events and the emotions attached to them. Later, I can look back at what I wrote from a more rational state of mind—rather than through the lens of my "reptilian brain" (the part that convinces me the world is ending at least once a day). Reading things from that calmer perspective often helps me realize I may have overreacted, and that maybe nobody actually hates me like I initially thought.

- **Becoming my own friend.** When I catch myself stuck in negative self-talk, I try to pause and respond the way I would to someone I love. I remind myself of my strengths, offer grace, and give myself the benefit of the doubt. I try to remember that being imperfect is part of being human, and that suffering isn't unique to me—everyone struggles sometimes.

- **Creating Myrtle.** While studying psychology, particularly Acceptance and Commitment Therapy (ACT), I learned about a concept called cognitive defusion: the ability to step back from your thoughts and see them as just that—thoughts, not facts.[1] One way to make thoughts less realistic is to make them more comical in nature. How can we do this? By making up a character with a distinct voice that represents those unkind thoughts. Myrtle is my character. She's an irritating, grumpy old lady who exists to make my life miserable. She wears ugly plum-colored lipstick and has a nasally, drawn out voice. Now, when I notice her intruding, I try to vividly imagine her character and then I tell her to zip it.

- **Allowing rest days.** I used to try to do as much as possible, every single day. I downloaded habit tracker apps, bought a plethora of planners, and packed my to-do lists in an effort to feel productive. But I was spreading myself too thin—and the worst part was that when I didn't accomplish everything I set out to do, I beat myself up over it. Rather than setting myself up for success, I kept chasing my own unreasonable expectations. What a perfect recipe for burnout. Now, I choose just a few priorities each day and celebrate the small wins. I also allow myself to have low-capacity days. Sometimes, doing nothing *is* self-care. Letting myself rest without guilt is an act of self-compassion.

- **Body check-ins.** I care for myself by bringing more awareness to my body. Throughout the day, I try to pause and ask myself what I need in that moment—it might be water, movement, stillness, quiet, or grounding. Body signals exist to let us know what we need to thrive, and tuning into this sometimes takes practice.

- **Reframing difficulties.** Before I knew I was autistic, I saw my difficulties as evidence that I was weak—but that's because I was measuring myself against neurotypical standards. Now, I understand that my needs aren't shortcomings; they're just needs, unique to my wiring. I try to use hard moments as data points to reflect on and learn from. We all thrive under different conditions, and some of us have to unlearn what we thought we should need in order to discover what we actually do.

- **Creating comforting rituals.** My favorite way to mentally recharge at the end of the day is by indulging in my own version of sensory bliss. Every evening, I take a hot shower, put on one of my softest pajama sets, and curl up under my favorite blanket, where I immerse myself in one of my hobbies: usually reading or cozy gaming. This ritual has become an essential part of my routine. It fills my cup and helps me feel ready to face the next day. More than just relaxing, it offers a sense of comforting familiarity that I can count on, especially when the day has been chaotic.

Every step that I take towards self compassion is an action that requires effort —it's not something that just comes naturally. I may have written a book, and I may have collected helpful strategies over the years that are guiding me toward a more peaceful, joy-filled life, but I am still in the midst of my own healing.

Stopping a pattern that's been hard-wired into my brain for so long, whether it's a thought loop, a critical inner voice, or a deeply ingrained belief, isn't a one-time decision. It's an ongoing, intentional, and often forceful interruption of beliefs I've come to recognize as not only harmful, but untrue.

So if you, reader, are on your own journey toward self-love, know this: healing is not linear—and that's okay.

Transforming deeply held beliefs takes far more than a list of tips and tricks. It takes presence, patience, and the courage to challenge what no longer serves you.

Don't forget to give yourself grace.

Autistic Joy: Naming the Light Within

My 3-year-old son, Lincoln, has a growing collection of Dr. Seuss books. It all started with *Fox in Socks*. The first time we read it together resulted in belly laughs and an immediate, "Let's read it again!"

More recently, I added *Oh, the Thinks You Can Think!* to his shelf. After reading it for him one morning, I was struck with memories of the very first musical theater production I'd done when I was just 12 years old—*Seussical the Musical*. The opening number instantly began playing in my head: *Oh the thinks you can think, think and wonder and dream, far and wide as you dare...*

So I did what I often do—I burst out in song and dance! There in my kitchen, I put on my own little performance. Lincoln was pretty used to me doing things like this. If anyone sees the fully unmasked version of me—the one that's wild, silly, and also a mess at times—it's him. So I don't always expect him to react. Yet this time, he surprised me with his interest. He watched me sing with wide, curious eyes, and slowly, a soft smile formed. "Mama, sing *Oh, the Thinks You Can Think*!" he pleaded when my performance came to a close.

"You want me to sing more?" I asked.

"Yeah," he answered quickly.

We had read, eaten breakfast, and planned to head out to the park next. "I have an idea," I told him. "I'll play the song for you in the car while we drive to the park. Does that sound good?"

He agreed. And if anything makes the transition from the house to the car less of a challenge, I'm game.

After I loaded up the kids and started up the car, I opened up Spotify on my phone and searched for the original Broadway soundtrack for *Seussical the Musical* and found the song. "Here it is," I told Lincoln.

I was just happy to find more music he enjoyed. Matt and I have been accumulating songs that end up in a playlist called "Lincoln's Playlist" since before he was one. It's been fun watching it evolve over time.

What I didn't expect was to feel the way I felt when I heard that opening song for the first time in years.

As the instrumentals trickled in, I began to watch my childhood experience replay inside my head. I saw myself backstage with my cast mates, waiting to emerge onto the stage. As the music built, I became flooded with nostalgia and felt myself drift off to that world—the one that was somehow still safely contained within my memories. In that moment, driving down the road with my little boy, it all came back to me vividly.

I turned down the volume for a second to ask Lincoln how he liked the song. He gave his approval, which made me smile. He had no idea, but somehow it felt like I was sharing a piece of my childhood with him. It was almost as if I was existing both as a girl and a woman at the same time, in the same space—like I was confronted with the bittersweet realization that time and age do not change who we have always been inside.

As the music continued, the joy of being transported to my memory only grew more intense. By the end of it, I found myself covered in goosebumps, my eyes wet with the hint of tears—three minutes and fifty-two seconds of euphoric happiness.

I have moments like this often. Moments when joy—over very simple things—fills my body to a level that can't be contained. I always felt that I was lucky to need so little to bring me happiness. I didn't know where it came from or why I was like this—until I heard about the term "autistic joy." Apparently, feeling happiness all the way down to your bones is common among autistics.

It makes a lot of sense, considering how we feel and sense everything else. Just like unpleasant feelings run deep, so does joy. It's just another way that autism can feel like a double-edged sword.

I experience autistic joy in a number of ways; these moments aren't always tied to memories in the same way that hearing a song can bring me back to another place in time.

I get a similar sort of excited energy when I dive into one of my special interests or a current hyperfixation. These topics or activities of strong interest are not only soothing, but energizing. Just *thinking* about them scratches some sort of itch inside my brain—and it feels *so* good. A free dopamine hit at any time.

I think what many people don't realize about special interests is that they're more than just hobbies we enjoy or things we obsess over. They're a source of motivation—sometimes even the very reason we get out of bed in the morning. They bring peace, purpose, and, most beautifully, what I'd call autistic joy.

Special interests aren't just something we think about when we finally have time to relax at the end of the day. They're threaded through our thoughts all day long. They show up in conversation, in the way we interpret the world, and in the little moments when our minds wander.

One of my more "fun" special interests is simulation games like *Stardew Valley* and *Animal Crossing*. When I'm especially hyperfixated, I catch myself thinking about them at random moments throughout the day. Maybe I'm mentally planning which in-game goals I'll tackle next, rearranging my virtual world in my head, or daydreaming about when I'll get to play again.

I might listen to game soundtracks or watch playthroughs while getting something done around the house. I might spend time online, looking at figurines, Lego sets, or guidebooks related to my favorite games.

In whatever way I welcome these interests into my day-to-day life, doing so fills me with fresh joy and excitement—it never seems to feel stale to me. And it amazes even me that a mere thought can boost my mood and bring me back to center, especially at times when my world feels uncomfortable or unpredictable.

As I mentioned in a previous chapter, my other special interests include autism (I know—not a surprise there), psychology, and neuroscience. I learn about these topics through research and reading. At any given time, I'm usually in the middle of a book that has something to do with one of these subjects.

My favorite part about learning is when I come across a finding that feels really profound—one that I want to lock away in my brain for safe keeping. The way the information clicks into place and opens up a new understanding of how humans work is truly invigorating to me, like a mental trip downhill on a rollercoaster.

One final way that I experience autistic joy is through how I internally experience the outside world, something I call sensory delight.

My favorite way to feel sensory delight is by engaging in my evening time cozy ritual, where I combine all the feelings I love into an indulgent, restorative time of deep relaxation. I change into clothes that don't feel so suffocating, spray on a sugary vanilla scent that makes me feel like I've just come out of a bakery, get under my blanket and pull it up to my chin, and read or game.

And *sometimes* (okay, a few times a week), my wonderful husband gives me a foot rub. This could easily be the best part of my day, because a simple foot rub, to me, might as well equate to a *spiritual experience*. I know that sounds far-fetched—but the feeling of deep pressure on my feet literally makes my whole body melt into relaxation at a level I can't duplicate in any other way. For me, it triggers something called an Autonomous Sensory Meridian Response (often referred to as ASMR).[1] The sensation feels like a brain massage of sorts—a fuzzy tingling in my head and ears, sometimes even traveling down my arms to my fingers. It's hard to describe, but it's an incredibly positive feeling and instantly makes me happy and at peace.

Sensory bliss can be experienced in a myriad of ways: in watching the trees rustle together in the wind, in smelling the first hint of crisp autumn air, in feeling the warmth of the sun my shoulders for the first time in months, in hearing a song that can be felt with my whole being.

All of these moments of heart-bursting joy are what make the ordinary parts of life feel like quiet celebrations unfolding inside of me, each and every day. Many times, it's the simple things that feel huge to me, while what feels exciting to others—parties, extravagant vacations, and big events—can just feel like *too much*.

This is what it means to live in a body wired for intensity. To feel everything. It's like riding through life on the back of a dragon—fierce, reactive, impossible to control. But slowly and painfully, over time, I'm learning to tame my dragon. To harness its power instead of fearing it.

Being different doesn't always feel empowering. It often feels dark, isolating, and confusing. I move through the world with a dull ache to be understood—and a deep hope that someday the world will wake with a longing to understand people like me, and care enough to try.

But now, I choose to let go. To leave behind this painful desire to be understood—and instead, to the best of my ability, just be me.

Because there has always been a light glowing beneath my surface, pulsing like breath. And although it has burned me, it has also allowed me to see the world in vivid color. To think deeply. To feel unearthly joy. To desire to learn and create. To love with everything that I am.

It's in those moments, when authentic joy rushes in and quiets the need to be anything but myself, that I come home to who I really am.

As I danced in the kitchen, belting out showtunes while my little boy looked at me like I was magic, I felt the present and past blur together—twelve-year-old me standing in stage lights, and the woman I've become now, lit up in a new way.

And in that moment, I realized: I've always been this girl. This self. She never left. She's still here—singing, feeling, reaching for joy.

Despite all the years I spent masking, doubting, and shrinking, I was being loved exactly as I am.

And that—all that pain and all that goodness—is the light I couldn't name.

Acknowledgments

To the One who fearfully and wonderfully made me—thank you, God, for weaving purpose into my story.

To my family, for walking beside me through every season.

To my partner in life and forever love, Matthew—thank you for your peace, patience, and unwavering support in all my endeavors, and for letting me infocump on you daily.

To my firstborn, Lincoln—loving you helped me love myself better. Being seen and loved by you when I'm fully unmasked has given me the courage to let others see me, too. You helped me return to the parts of me I had buried.

To my youngest son, Luca—you are truly my bringer of light and joy. You complete our family and remind me everyday to laugh and let go.

To my mom—for raising me to be a warrior queen. You saw it in me before I could.

And to the neurodivergent community—without your courage to share your stories, mine may never have been written. Thank you for propelling me forward with your support and for creating a safe space where I feel I truly belong.

Author Note

Writing this book has been healing in and of itself. Since my diagnosis, I have spent the past couple of years trying to unravel my past and connect the dots between autism and my internal experience. Going through it all in writing has allowed me to systematically process and understand things that were unclear for so long.

I've always said that I would publish a book one day, but I never knew that it would be about autism or my life. When I first got the idea, I treated it like journaling. *If it never goes anywhere, I'll have done it for me*, I thought.

In the book, I talk a few times about feeling this unrelenting, painful desire to be understood. That was my motivation; I simply wanted to provide deeper understanding for those on the outside, and validation for autistic individuals who present similarly to me.

Yet somehow, by the end of writing, I had finally let go of that need to be understood—not fully, but more than I ever have before. Just taking those brave steps in the right direction has been transformative. And now I'm walking away with something I am so proud of—for reasons deeper than the chase for approval or acceptance.

I wrote this book for the quiet little girl I once was—to show her that she had a bright light burning inside all along. But I also wrote it for women who discovered their neurodivergence later in life and are just now learning who they really are. And of course, I wrote it for the very special people who care enough to take an inside peek into my unique world.

My hope is to gently open others up to the idea of these nuanced presentations of autism. To cause others to stop and think before assuming that autism has a specific "look" or personality. To make space for those who are different.

Autism is not a superpower nor a tragedy. It's a neurotype, a way of being designed. And like I've said, it's certainly a double-edged sword.

I don't want to be separated from my autism. It is an integral part of what makes me the person that I am. It affects the way that I think, interact with others, learn, and sense. I always felt that my experience of life was different, in both difficult and profound ways. Autism is what best explains everything. And just knowing how to name it has made my view that much clearer.

To every reader who is neurodivergent: I see you. And though this story is one that ends on a positive note, just know that I am a work very much in progress. Some days feel unbearable. Others are bright and full. Sometimes I feel like the world is judging me by everything I do and say. Others, I am able to let go of the need to be liked. We are all growing and healing together—and sometimes we wither a bit before we bloom again, and that's okay.

My very best piece of advice today is not to cage yourself for the sake of other people. It's better not to be liked by everyone than to be imprisoned in your mind.

Endnotes

Introduction

1. Hull, L., Petrides, K. V., Allison, C., Smith, P., Baron-Cohen, S., Lai, M.-C., & Mandy, W. (2017). "Putting on My Best Normal": Social Camouflaging in Adults with Autism Spectrum Conditions. Journal of Autism and Developmental Disorders, 47(8), 2519–2534. https://doi.org/10.1007/s10803-017-3166-5

2. Cage, E., Di Monaco, J., & Newell, V. (2018). Experiences of Autism Acceptance and Mental Health in Autistic Adults. Journal of Autism and Developmental Disorders, 48(2), 473–484. https://doi.org/10.1007/s10803-017-3342-7

3. Solomon, A. (2023, June 22). Donald Triplett, 'Case 1' in Autism History, Dies at 89. The New York Times. https://www.nytimes.com/2023/06/22/health/donald-triplett-autism.html

Don't Worry, She's Just Shy

1. Zwaigenbaum, L., Bauman, M. L., Choueiri, R., Kasari, C., Carter, A., Granpeesheh, D., ... & Natowicz, M. R. (2015). Early identification and interventions for autism spectrum disorder: Executive summary. Pediatrics, 136(Supplement 1), S1–S9. ht tps://doi.org/10.1542/peds.2014-3667B

2. Swanson MR, Shen MD, Wolff JJ, Boyd B, Clements M, Rehg J, Elison JT, Paterson S, Parish-Morris J, Chappell JC, Hazlett HC, Emerson RW, Botteron K, Pandey J, Schultz RT, Dager SR, Zwaigenbaum L, Estes AM, Piven J; IBIS Network. Naturalistic Language Recordings Reveal "Hypervocal" Infants at High Familial Risk for Autism. Child Dev. 2018 Mar;89(2):e60-e73. doi: 10.1111/cdev.12777. Epub 2017 Mar 10. PMID: 28295208; PMCID: PMC5592123.

3. Werling, D. M., & Geschwind, D. H. (2013). Sex differences in autism spectrum disorders. Current Opinion in Neurology, 26(2), 146–153. https://doi.org/10.1097/WCO.0b013e3283 5ee548

4. Grigorenko, E. L., Klin, A., & Volkmar, F. (2003). Annotation: Hyperlexia: Disability or superability? Journal of Child Psychology and Psychiatry, 44(8), 1079–1091. https://doi.org /10.1111/1469-7610.00191

New Surroundings, Old Sensitivities

1. Velázquez & Galán, Information gain in the brain's resting state: A new perspective on autism, Frontiers in Neuroinformatics (2013).

The Year My Body Said No

1. Raymaker, D. M., Teo, A. R., Steckler, N. A., Lentz, B., Schillawski, J., & Nicolaidis, C. (2020). "Having all of your internal resources exhausted beyond measure and being left with no clean-up crew": Defining autistic burnout. Autism in Adulthood, 2(2), 132–143. https://doi.org/10.1089/aut.2019.0079

2. Higgins, K. (2022, September 15). What is autistic burnout? Charlie Health. https://www.charliehealth.com/post/what-is-autistic-burnout

3. Sellers, R. (2023, February 21). What is autistic burnout? Verywell Mind. https://www.verywellmind.com/what-is-autistic-burnout-7482093

Rivers of Wonder

1. American Psychiatric Association. (2022). Diagnostic and statistical manual of mental disorders (5th ed., text rev.; DSM-5-TR). https://doi.org/10.1176/appi.books.9780890425787

2. Cook, A., Ogden, J., & Winstone, N. (2021). Friendship motivations, challenges and the role of masking for autistic and neurotypical adolescents. Journal of Autism and Developmental Disorders, 51(3), 848–861. https://doi.org/10.1007/s10803-0 20-04579-4

3. Murray, D., Lesser, M., & Lawson, W. (2005). Attention, monotropism and the diagnostic criteria for autism. Autism, 9(2), 139–156. https://doi.org/10.1177/1362361305051398

4. Woods, R. (2023). Monotropism: An organizing principle for understanding autism. Autism, 27(3), 790–803. https://doi.or g/10.1177/13623613221149410

The Autistic Analyst

1. Behavior Analyst Certification Board. (2020). Professional and Ethical Compliance Code for Behavior Analysts. https://www.bacb.com/wp-content/uploads/2020/11/BACB-Compliance-Code-english_190318.pdf

2. Horner, R. H., Sugai, G., & Lewis, T. J. (2015). Is school-wide positive behavior support an evidence-based practice? Center on Positive Behavioral Interventions and Supports. https://www.pbis.org/resource/is-school-wide-positive-behavior-support-an-evidence-based-practice

3. Leaf, J. B., Cihon, J. H., Ferguson, J. L., Milne, C., Leaf, R., McEachin, J., & Weiss, M. J. (2021). ABA is a science and, therefore, progressive. Journal of Autism and Developmental Disorders, 51(12), 4326–4330. https://doi.org/10.1007/s1080 3-020-04773-5

4. Sandoval-Norton, A. H., & Shkedy, G. (2019). How much compliance is too much compliance: Is long-term ABA therapy abuse? Cogent Psychology, 6(1), 1641258. https://doi.org/10. 1080/23311908.2019.1641258

5. Kupferstein, H. (2018). Evidence of increased PTSD symptoms in autistics exposed to applied behavior analysis. Advances in Autism, 4(1), 19–29. https://doi.org/10.1108/AIA-08-201 7-0016

6. Bottema-Beutel, K., Crowley, S., Sandbank, M., & Woynaroski, T. (2021). Research review: Conflicts of interest (COIs) in autism early intervention research – a meta-analysis of COI prevalence and associations with effect size. Journal of Child Psychology and Psychiatry, 62(1), 5–15. https://doi.org/10.11 11/jcpp.13204

No Filter

1. STAR Institute for Sensory Processing. (n.d.). Your 8 Senses. Retrieved from STAR Institute website.

2. Lieberman, M. D., Inagaki, T. K., Tabibnia, G., & Crockett, M. J. (2007). Putting feelings into words: Affect labeling disrupts amygdala activity to affective stimuli. Psychological Science, 18(5), 421–428.

3. Yoshimura, S., Shimomura, K., & Onoda, K. (2024). Diminished negative emotion regulation through affect labeling and reappraisal: Insights from functional near infrared spectroscopy. BMC Psychology, 12, 613.

Probably Don't Throw Me a Surprise Party

1. American Psychiatric Association. (2013). *Diagnostic and Statistical Manual of Mental Disorders (5th ed.)*. https://doi.org/10.1176/appi.books.9780890425596

2. *Perseverate* means to repeat a thought or action long after the stimulus that prompted it has ended. In autism, it often refers to getting mentally "stuck" on a specific idea or emotion.

3. Najmi, S., Riemann, B. C., Wegner, D. M., & Nock, M. K. (2009). Implicit self-regulation in obsessive-compulsive disorder: Neutralizing implicit distressing thoughts. *Behaviour Research and Therapy, 47*(6), 494–498. https://doi.org/10.1016/j.brat.2009.03.001

Running Low on Spoons

1. Diamond, A. (2013). Executive functions. Annual Review of Psychology, 64, 135–168. https://doi.org/10.1146/annurev-psych-113011-143750

2. Leitner, Y. (2014). The co-occurrence of autism and attention deficit hyperactivity disorder in children – what do we know? Frontiers in Human Neuroscience, 8, 268. https://doi.org/10.3389/fnhum.2014.0026

3. Volkow, N. D., Wang, G. J., Newcorn, J. H., Kollins, S. H., Wigal, T. L., Telang, F., ... & Swanson, J. M. (2011). Motivation deficit in ADHD is associated with dysfunction of the dopamine reward pathway. Molecular Psychiatry, 16(11), 1147–1154. https://doi.org/10.1038/mp.2010.97

4. Miserandino, C. M. (2003). The Spoon Theory. But You Don't Look Sick. https://butyoudontlooksick.com/articles/written-by-christine/the-spoon-theory/

The People Pleasing Paradox

1. Newson, E. (2014). Pathological demand avoidance syndrome: My daughter is not naughty. Jessica Kingsley Publishers.

2. Christie, P., & Vague, A. (2018). Rethinking Pathological

Demand Avoidance: Towards a more respectful understanding. Journal of Autism and Developmental Disorders, 48(7), 2347–2355. https://doi.org/10.1007/s10803-018-3570-4

3. Happé, F., & Frith, U. (2020). Annual Research Review: Looking back to look forward – changes in the concept of autism and implications for future research. Journal of Child Psychology and Psychiatry, 61(3), 218–232. https://doi.org/10.1111/j cpp.13124

Out of Sight, Not Out of Heart

1. American Psychiatric Association. (2013). Diagnostic and statistical manual of mental disorders (5th ed.). https://doi.or g/10.1176/appi.books.9780890425596

2. Crompton, C. J., Ropar, D., Evans-Williams, C. V. M., Flynn, E. G., & Fletcher-Watson, S. (2020). Autistic peer-to-peer information transfer is highly effective. Autism, 24(7), 1704–1712. https://doi.org/10.1177/1362361320919286

3. Mottron, L., Dawson, M., Soulières, I., Hubert, B., & Burack, J. (2006). Enhanced perceptual functioning in autism: An update, and eight principles of autistic perception. Journal of Autism and Developmental Disorders, 36(1), 27–43. https://doi.org/10.1007/s10803-005-0040-7

4. Barkley, R. A. (2012). Executive functions: What they are, how they work, and why they evolved. Guilford Press.

The Diagnosis

1. O'Nions, E., Viding, E., Greven, C. U., Ronald, A., & Happé, F. (2014). Pathological demand avoidance: Exploring the behavioural profile. Autism, 18(5), 538–544. https://doi.org/10.117 7/1362361313481634

2. Volkow, N. D., Wang, G. J., Fowler, J. S., & Tomasi, D. (2011). Addiction circuitry in the human brain. Annual Review of Pharmacology and Toxicology, 52, 321–336. https://doi.or g/10.1146/annurev-pharmtox-010611-134625

3. Baron-Cohen, S., Wheelwright, S., Skinner, R., Martin, J., & Clubley, E. (2001). The Autism Spectrum Quotient (AQ): Evidence from Asperger Syndrome/high-functioning autism, males and females, scientists and mathematicians. Journal of Autism and Developmental Disorders, 31(1), 5–17. https://d oi.org/10.1023/A:1005653411471
Ritvo, R. A., Ritvo, E. R., Guthrie, D., Ritvo, M. J., Hufnagel, D. H., McMahon, W., ... & Eloff, J. (2011). The Ritvo Autism Asperger Diagnostic Scale–Revised (RAADS–R): A scale to assist the diagnosis of Autism Spectrum Disorder in adults: An international validation study. Journal of Autism and Developmental Disorders, 41(8), 1076–1089. https://doi.org/10.1007

/s10803-010-1133-5

Hull, L., Mandy, W., Lai, M. C., Baron-Cohen, S., Allison, C., Smith, P., & Petrides, K. V. (2019). Development and validation of the Camouflaging Autistic Traits Questionnaire (CAT-Q). Journal of Autism and Developmental Disorders, 49(3), 819–833. https://doi.org/10.1007/s10803-018-3792-6

4. Hehir, T. (2002). Eliminating ableism in education. Harvard Educational Review, 72(1), 1–32. https://doi.org/10.17763/h aer.72.1.03866528702g2105

Freefalling

1. Livingston, L. A., Shah, P., & Happé, F. (2020). Compensatory strategies below the surface in autism: A qualitative study. The Lancet Psychiatry, 7(9), 788–796.

2. Hull, L., Petrides, K. V., Allison, C., Smith, P., Baron-Cohen, S., Lai, M. C., & Mandy, W. (2019). "Putting on My Best Normal": Social Camouflaging in Adults with Autism Spectrum Conditions. Journal of Autism and Developmental Disorders, 49(2), 704–716.

The Art of Movement

1. Kapp, S. K., Steward, R., Crane, L., Elliott, D., Elphick, C., Pellicano, E., & Milton, D. (2019). 'People should be allowed to do what they like': Autistic adults' views and experiences of

stimming. Autism, 23(7), 1782–1792. https://doi.org/10.117
7/1362361319829628

2. Blanc, M. (2020). Natural Language Acquisition on the
Autism Spectrum: The Journey from Echolalia to Self-Gener-
ated Language. Meaningful Speech.

Unfixable

1. Baron-Cohen, S., Wheelwright, S., Skinner, R., Martin, J.,
& Clubley, E. (2001). The Autism Spectrum Quotient (AQ):
Evidence from Asperger Syndrome/high-functioning autism,
males and females, scientists and mathematicians. Journal of
Autism and Developmental Disorders, 31(1), 5–17. https://d
oi.org/10.1023/A:1005653411471

2. Porges, S. W. (2011). The polyvagal theory: Neurophysiolog-
ical foundations of emotions, attachment, communication, and
self-regulation. W. W. Norton & Company.

The Quest for Self Compassion

1. Hayes, S. C., Strosahl, K. D., & Wilson, K. G. (2016). Acceptance and commitment therapy: The process and practice of
mindful change (2nd ed.). Guilford Press.

Autistic Joy

1. Barratt, E. L., & Davis, N. J. (2015). Autonomous Sensory Meridian Response (ASMR): A flow-like mental state. PeerJ, 3, e851. https://doi.org/10.7717/peerj.851

www.ingramcontent.com/pod-product-compliance
Lightning Source LLC
Chambersburg PA
CBHW031458120626
46545CB00005B/1660